THE POLITICS OF COMMUNITY POLICING

CURRENT ISSUES IN CRIMINAL JUSTICE
VOLUME 25
GARLAND REFERENCE LIBRARY OF SOCIAL SCIENCE
VOLUME 1179

THE POLITICS OF
COMMUNITY POLICING
THE CASE OF SEATTLE

WILSON EDWARD REED

GARLAND PUBLISHING, INC.
A MEMBER OF THE TAYLOR & FRANCIS GROUP
NEW YORK AND LONDON
1999

Library of Congress Cataloging-in-Publication Data

Reed, Wilson Edward.
    The politics of community policing : the case of Seattle / by Wilson
Edward Reed.
        p.   cm. — (Garland reference library of social science ; v. 1179.
Current issues in criminal justice ; v. 25)
    Includes bibliographical references and index.
    ISBN 0-8153-3029-4 (alk. paper)
    1. Community policing—Washington (State)—Seattle.   2. Law enforce-
ment—Washington (State)—Seattle.   3. Seattle (Wash.)—Social conditions.   4. Seattle (Wash.)—Politics and government.   I. Title.   II. Series:
Garland reference library of social science ; v. 1179.   III. Series: Garland
reference library of social science. Current issues in criminal justice ; v. 25.
HV7936.C83R44   1999
363.2'3'09797772—dc21   98-45478
                                                                                  CIP

Cover photograph of West Precinct Bicycle Squad Officers at Harborview
Viewpoint. Photograph by Officer Terri MacMillan, used by permission of the
Seattle Police Department.

Printed on acid-free, 250-year-life paper
Manufactured in the United States of America

Contents

Series Editors' Foreword

Although the wide-scale implementation of various forms of community policing throughout the last two decades has probably led us no closer to the resolution of the fundamental questions about the "impossible" police mandate, the prioritization of goals and the allocation of diminishing resources, it is remarkable for its popularity and political utility. Any movement of mass appeal, such as community policing, seems to generate from a particular set of sociopolitical conditions which may tell us as much about our process of problem-solving as our values and ideals. In this work, Edward Reed details the mechanics of the community policing experience in Seattle. Because of the scope of the community policing experience, the characters and the events of this work probably parallel those of other cities and towns all across America. In a very comprehensive analysis Reed explores the effect of the community policing package on the citizen, on citizen groups, on the police organization and on the greater political system.

As with the other volumes in this series, readers will appreciate the clear and compelling way this case study is presented. Reed critiques the way in which political and economic dynamics not only threaten, but convolute the intended benefits of community policing. Although you may not always agree with the author's interpretations, he has given us a compelling look at the potential for corruption of model programs. This work rounds out the work on policing in this series and nicely complements previous volumes by Bernadette Palombo and Otwin Marenin.

Marilyn D. McShane
Frank P. Williams III

Preface

Community policing is an increasingly influential approach to law enforcement that has been defined by its proponents as a model partnership between citizens and police. The basic characteristic of community policing in its radical form is personalized policing where a given officer patrols the same area on a permanent basis, operates from a decentralized mini-station or storefront, and works with citizens to identify and solve crime problems. This study examines how the police department in Seattle, Washington, maneuvered through political pressures to create what has come to be defined as a model for community policing, and it asks how closely this model program fits the ideal of community policing.

It is suggested that the shift to a community policing model occurred because of the perceived failure of traditional police control strategies, which were aimed at slowing the crime rate. Moreover, the actual practice of community policing in Seattle was the result of the interaction between the community and police department politics, rather than the simple bureaucratic implementation of a rational strategy of crime control.

This analysis utilizes three theoretical approaches to understand and illuminate the politics of community policing in Seattle, Washington, from 1985 to 1993. First, legitimation theory is used to analyze the broader fiscal issues of the state government. Sidney Harring (1983) professes that the legitimation function of the police is important because it has an internal effect as well as an external one. Moreover, the police institution gains legitimacy when it makes some accommodations to the communities being policed.

Second, urban political processes are used to address the social and political issues of Seattle, such as crime increases, drugs, and street crime. Finally, micro-organizational processes provide insight into how traditional bureaucratic organizations resist change, adapt, negotiate, compromise, or co-opt crime control strategies in concert with neighborhood and community-based organizations. Peter K. Manning (1977:139) helps one understand the police organization. He notes that "organizations are in many ways constituted as a series of negotiated situations in which persons acting within organizational roles confront and make sense of a shared event."

Using Seattle as an example, it is apparent that multiple political and economic forces shape policing strategies, and that police departments are placed in a reactive mode when called upon to manage and control crises and pressures not of their making in large metropolitan cities. This case study concluded that political pressure from community groups played an important role in shaping the variant of community policing eventually implemented in Seattle. Evidence uncovered from this study showed that community policing teams were highly symbolic and political rather than meaningful agents of crime control and prevention.

THE POLITICS OF
COMMUNITY POLICING

CHAPTER 1

Introduction

COMMUNITY POLICING TO THE RESCUE

> It is time for America to make a serious commitment to community policing, to having people back on the beat, working the same neighborhoods, making relationships with people in ways that prevent crime.
>
> Bill Clinton, Detroit, Michigan, October 17, 1992

In 1992, candidate Bill Clinton gave national recognition to the concept of community policing during his presidential campaign. As president of the United States, he has tried to sell it as one solution to the crime problem, and has credited community policing as one of the reasons for the downward turn in crime statistics.

Community policing has been described by some politicians, academicians, and law enforcement officials as the solution to the crime problem in the United States. Trojanowicz (1991) contends that community-oriented policing curbs police brutality. He argues that if the Los Angeles Police Department had a true form of community policing, it could have avoided the Rodney King incident. Goldstein (1993) claims that it is inconceivable that a police officer imbued with community policing would engage in the type of behavior illustrated in the beating of Rodney King.

Trojanowicz (1992) indicates that the United States needs a fundamental change in the relationship between people and the police. Furthermore, he states that only community policing can supply the necessary major shift from confrontation to cooperation. Hundreds of cities across the United States have experimented with putting police officers back on neighborhood foot patrols and into storefronts and mini-stations in the name of community policing. Police and community residents have formed partnerships to do something about persistent street-level crime and disorder. However, while there has been considerable promotion of the idea and philosophy of community policing, far less has been written about its actual practice.

This study reveals how one police department subtly managed external and internal pressures to develop a model community policing program. Policy makers will find the research helpful in understanding political and economic structures, urban politics, and police organizations as they seek to gain consent and legitimacy in neighborhoods and communities where relationships are fragile and conflictual. Scholars will find the research helpful in understanding how public officials use symbolic labels in ways that increase public expectations of the police. Community residents and local leaders will find that "community control" of the police is a faint whisper in the wind for radicals and progressives who want change in police departments. This creates an impression that community policing will provide an instant solution for the problem of crime and racial tensions (Goldstein, 1993).

POLITICS OF COMMUNITY POLICING

Skolnick (1971) notes that police departments are social organizations created and sustained by *political processes*. This understanding of policing requires a sensitivity to the politics underlying the police organization. Furthermore, Bayley (1985) argues that police affect political processes, not only by what they do, but also by what they do not do.

The politics of community policing have been discussed by Manning (1984), Walker (1984), and Klockars (1985) in Greene and Mastrofski's *Community Policing: Rhetoric or Reality* (1988). The politics of community policing presume that poor inner city residents desire close contact with police departments, especially crime control activities that are driven by police-community relations experts. It is argued that the politics of community policing concern the police department subtly maintaining consent and legitimacy. Community policing is described by these authors as an ideological construct to maintain social control in a postmodern society filled with social ills and major fiscal problems.

Defining Community

Before one can consider the nature of community policing, it is necessary to know what is meant by the idea of community. Strecher (1991:78) raises an important question that is tangential to this study: "Where is community?" He notes that "an 'American community' is a warm, comforting phrase." He also says, "In this concept there is an overtone of the small society—the community of neighbors who know each other (to the third generation), and whose offspring develop their self-awareness in an atmosphere of warmth, trust and a wish to become like those who have gone before . . . 'Community' is a realization of the romanticized melting pot." Many people wish the above statement could be true. However, the reality is that there are many individuals with different needs and goals looking out for themselves. Community policing ideally would draw these people together to form a community where all would get along and look out for each other in the fight against street crime and criminals.

Likewise, Klockars (1988:247-248) discusses the mystification of the concept of community. He states, "The concept of community implies a group of people with a common history, common beliefs and understandings, a sense of themselves as 'us' and outsiders as 'them,' and often, but not always, a shared territory." Greene and Mastrofski (1988:xii) note that the community is viewed as an active agent in social change when people speak about community policing. The police are, in part, responsible for activating the community to act and solve problems in its own self-interest. The author of this research defines community as a social organization that provides for its members in totality.

Several policing scholars are critical of the commercial definitions of "community" and "community policing" in general. Klockars (1988) criticizes the definitions of community offered by early community policing advocates and argues that the movement could best be understood as the latest in a fairly long line of circumlocutions whose purpose is to conceal, mystify, and legitimate police distribution of non-negotiable force. There is considerable debate and conflict between pro-community advocates and those who argue that there is no "community." Thus, the definition of community continues to evolve and to be a source of debate for advocates of community-oriented policing (Goldstein, 1993). The only real problem with so many different definitions of "community" is that when it comes time to design a community policing program, any police strategy could be implemented and called "community" policing. Therefore, there is no consistent baseline from which to begin to design, implement, and evaluate the program(s).

Defining Politics

Politics is defined in an interdisciplinary manner throughout this research. Generally, political scientists define politics as an allocative process. Politics is defined in this study as the process by which authoritative decisions are made about who gets what, when, and how in society (Easton, 1965:50). Sociologists, in contrast, define politics as the exercise of constraint in any social relationship. Both political scientists and sociologists agree that politics is potentially present in all social relationships, in that politics essentially involves the exercise of power.

Politics is integral to any police operation and involves the exercise of influence and power. According to Alpert and Dunham (1988:78), "Community politics involve democratic control over the policing function. A fundamental value of our society is that policing should be subject to and under some control of the public."

The politics of community policing has both internal and external dimensions in urban police departments (Manning, 1977; Harring, 1983). An example of an internal dimension would be if the police chief offers resistance to community policing strategies. An external dimension is the pressure from the neighborhood groups and organizations to do something about street crime in their district. Community politics involve democratic control over the policing function. Alpert and Dunham (1988) believe that internal and external politics are intertwined. They state:

> As various community agencies and organizations compete for influence and power over the policing function, external politics become interwoven with internal politics to produce a complex network of influences and power. Even though many police chiefs have vowed to keep politics out of their police departments, it is nearly an impossibility. (p. 69)

The politics of community policing may encompass practices, programs, and approaches to manage communities and neighborhoods whose support for the police organization appears to be weak or non-existent (Brogden, 1982; Reiner, 1985; Scraton, 1985; Gordon, 1987).

In spite of considerable indication of a high level of support for the police organization by the community, there is substantive evidence of the tentative and stratified features of this local support (Brogden, 1982). Even though the majority of citizens have a positive view of the police and support them, this support is not uniform across all segments of society and in all social settings. For example, a study by Albrecht and Green in 1977 on the attitudes toward police found that older citizens view the police more positively than younger citizens, white citizens view the police more positively than minority citizens, and people from lower socioeconomic groups are more likely to view the police negatively than middle- and upper-class groups (Kappeler et al., 1994). Therefore, it is clear that different groups have differing views of the police, their conduct, and the services they provide (Kappeler et al., 1994).

In recognition of the fragility of consent, the police institution is constantly forced to reconstruct consensual relations with the social classes in society. Brogden (1982) states that police service, in its various manifestations, has recently been given added weight as the major device for creating consent. The politics of community policing entails securing the governability of rising urban populations that are fractured along multiple lines of tension, including those of class and race (Websdale, 1991).

The central argument of this study is that community policing is a way of policing social and economic class divisions so as to avoid the serious public conflicts that have plagued policing in recent years (Brogden et al., 1988). The goal of this research is to provide an analysis of the way in which the *actual* practice of community policing in Seattle resulted from an interaction between the community and the police department, rather than the simple bureaucratic implementation of a rational crime control strategy by the department. This analysis is based on close examination of the interplay between top-down versus bottom up policing in the city since 1985. Top-down policing means that those who have authorized expertise make critical decisions for local residents. In bottom up policing, citizens receiving service assistance set priorities and influence police policy (Trojanowicz and Bucqueroux, 1994:3). Many new activities purporting to be true community policing are in fact old police-community relations programs. This examination also attempts to determine if some citizens in Seattle were over-policed and unprotected in certain pockets of the city, as some critics of the police department claimed (Gossett, 1993). The reader needs to understand that it is possible to be over-policed and under-protected at the same time. It should be pointed out that in this study, community policing efforts will be discussed only as they pertain to two areas in Seattle, the south end (a.k.a. Rainier Valley) and the central district (Appendix A).

COMMUNITY POLICING

Community policing means many things to many people. It is sometimes said to include elements of foot patrol, vertical patrol, mini-stations, storefront centers, special purpose patrol, fear reduction efforts, premise-security crime-prevention programs, citizen patrol, problem-oriented policing, location-oriented policing, and a variety of other operations (Strecher, 1991). Community policing is personalized policing that involves the same officer patrolling the same area on a permanent basis, operating from a decentralized mini-station or storefront, and working with citizens to identify and solve crime problems (Trojanowicz and Bucqueroux, 1994:3). In this same vein, police cannot be community police unless the institution and the officers are of and in that community (Robinson et al., 1994). Bayley (1988:225) says, "Community policing is the new philosophy of professional law enforcement in the world's industrialized democracies .... Wherever change is occurring, community policing is the watchword."

In *Community Policing: How To Get Started* (1994), Trojanowicz and Bucqueroux contend that it is the police chief and local political officials who should have the final say in the new citizen-police partnership. Specifically, the authors contend that it is the chief who should lead the charge in making the transition to community policing within the police organization. This is logical, because there is enormous pressure on police chiefs to do something about the street crime problem. Bouza (1990:31) notes that "today's police chief, pressured and harried to produce safety in an unsafe society, is increasingly reaching out to enlist the citizen's aid in the struggle." He adds that this reaching out "flies in the face of police insularity, separateness, and secrecy, and it is hard to know how sincerely even the chiefs have embraced the new idea" of community policing.

Community policing should be a process whereby police get out of their cars and take seriously those issues which are nominated by the citizens who are impacted by street crime (Reed, 1995). However, some police experts contend that the process of nominating problems might be less citizen-directed and more police-directed. Certainly the solutions are police-generated. For example, the policing of "hot spots" is generated by police executives rather than citizens.

Citizen-Police Partnerships

Widespread public support exists for police department decentralization, permanent assignments, and the development of citizen-police partnerships with local communities (Goldstein, 1993:2). Goldstein states that partnerships are activities that the police and community members enter into to solve problems of interest to both parties. A number of departments have attempted to define what partnership policing means in theory and practice. Partnership policing in Seattle, for instance, has been defined as a working relationship with residents and neighbors to achieve the mission of the department (Fleissner et al., 1992:1). However, achieving the mission of the department is more of a police concern than a community-nominated issue.

In theory, community policing necessarily requires a radical reformation of what police do and have done traditionally. Because full adoption of community policing would involve substantial organizational change, including the leveling of the bureaucratic hierarchy, one can expect resistance to such changes from within a police department. For instance, McConville and Shepherd (1992) discovered that British efforts to employ community policing came into conflict with the rank-and-file police culture that celebrates aggression, machismo, and the assertion of authority. This resistance is traceable to earlier police innovations and/or approaches such as team policing: "Team policing . . . gave powers to the bottom that had traditionally been reserved for the middle. Thus team policing was a form of decentralization which gave less power to mid-management. . . . As a result, middle management often impeded their administrators' goals for team policing." (Sherman et al., 1973:91)

This tension brought on by change is further heightened and complicated by strong public demands that police do something about the crime problem. At times these demands may be contradictory; that is, different sectors of the public may prefer different police practices as it relates to controlling street crime. Thus, in addressing the crime problem, police departments often find themselves negotiating among multiple political pressures emanating from the public and from their own internal politics. Williams and Wagoner (1995:366) note that police can be proactive, specifically, when "in response to internal pressures from top administration, which is often acting in response to external pressures" to do something about crime.

Klockars (1994) says that police cannot do much about the social problems that engulf most communities. Nevertheless, police chiefs and administrators whose jobs are constantly on the line feel pressures to fix street-level problems, such as public drug dealing, prostitution, and drive-by shootings (Bouza, 1990).

Goldstein (1990) develops the concept of problem-oriented policing and suggests that the police practices and strategies should strike a balance between reactive and proactive aspects of policing. He indicates that problem-solving policing creates a vehicle for making more effective use of the community and rank-and-file officers in getting the police job done. In its broadest context, problem-solving is a comprehensive plan for improving policing and addressing substantive problems shaping the police agency and influencing all changes in personnel, organization, and procedures.

Goldstein's definition of problem-oriented policing ties the police agency to the larger community. Allegedly, the community is a co-partner in problem solving and actively participates with grassroots organizations and leaders. Police officers become change agents dealing with a host of community problems and issues. Goldstein (1993) argues that police must give more substance to community policing by getting more involved in analyzing and responding to the specific problems citizens bring to their attention. Basically, the difference between community policing and problem-solving policing is that community policing seeks to establish long-term relationships with residents, and problem-solving policing is based on solving persistent and nagging community problems and moving on to new projects. A key assumption of community policing has been that ordinary citizens can take effective action, if properly directed and organized, to reduce the incidence of crime. According to Bayley (1994), up to this point, research has not supported this assumption.

Skolnick and Bayley (1986) reviewed research on traditional policing and conducted interviews in six United States cities. They indicate that community policing is not a technique or a program; it involves a customer focus embracing a philosophy that will provide a high quality service. Also, they note that it is not a limited or specialized style of policing. They suggest that it is full-service policing, giving attention to 911 calls plus proactive style prevention. They intimate that community policing is not foot patrol or riding a bicycle. Furthermore, community policing is much more than walking or cruising a neighborhood or a business area. They indicate that community policing involves an officer becoming knowledgeable of the area and familiar with the residents and business people. Most of all, community policing incorporates problem-solving approaches ranging from working with organized neighborhood associations to making referrals to other community resource services.

In the preface to *Community Policing: Rhetoric or Reality* (1988:xi), Greene and Mastrofski define community policing as a current trend that stresses a "contextual role for the police, one that emphasizes greater interaction with the community toward the resolution of persistent community problems alleged to lead to crime and social disorder." The above statement is typical for the time in which it was written. Its focus is more on the police role in crime prevention in the community than on community-directed anti-crime initiatives.

Scheingold (1991:76) defines community policing as the "notion that the police mission has as much to do with social service as with crime control." He indicates that community policing calls upon street-level officers to develop close relationships with their neighborhoods and to work through local community organizations rather than claim a monopoly on public service activities. This definition is apropos, as it brings the community into the process as an equal partner with the police in the fight against crime and disorder.

In McElroy, Cosgrove, and Sadd's (1993:7) discussion of the Brooklyn Police Department's Community Patrol Officer Program, the authors quote the Brooklyn Police Department's definition of community policing as "a philosophical position holding that the goals of policing, the conditions it addresses, the service it delivers, and the assessments of its adequacy should be formulated and developed in recognition of the distinctive experiences, needs, and norms of local communities." These authors realize that all communities and neighborhoods could not be similarly policed. They argue that diversified policing does not have to be differential policing in practice.

Overall, having so many diverse definitions confuses proponents of community policing. The various definitions by community policing scholars are all advantageous, but when a police department wants to begin a community policing program, it does not have a concrete set of operational procedures to follow. Therefore, a police department can establish its own procedures and programs and call it community policing, problem-oriented policing, partnership policing, etc. One possible benefit of so many definitions is that the program can be interpreted differently by every police department and tailored to fit that particular department's needs. In attempts to design a.d implement a community policing program, departments have visited other departments around the country to observe their implementation of community policing. The sharing and observing of ideas and philosophies is a benefit. The one major drawback of having no universal set of procedures is that there is no formal way to evaluate the effectiveness of community policing in target neighborhoods.

Major Assumptions of Community Policing

There are some major assumptions embedded in the philosophy and practice of community policing that overstate what the police have the capability to do and understate the role of citizen groups' involvement in crime reduction and control. Many of these assumptions are controversial because they changed the role of the police from proactive to reactive. For years, minority citizens and inner city residents have been fighting for community control of the police and for police to take seriously the issues and concerns nominated by citizen groups. Some community advocates are leery of the rhetoric flowing from the police department and wonder about the true motivation of the department.

Policing reforms of the 1990s are not simple, bureaucratic responses to rational ideas. They are the outcomes of complicated political processes and pressures. To understand the actual forms of community policing, one needs to examine the underlying political processes and pressures that shape them in practice. Riechers and Roberg (1990:107) have developed a list of the ten most prominent underlying assumptions of community policing. The purpose of presenting the assumptions is to illustrate how these assumptions are symbolic and sometimes fabricated.

- *Assumption 1.* The presence of the police through increased visibility reduces the public's fear of crime.

Early community policing critics argued that many groups in society do not desire an expanded police presence. The nature of the demand for police service depends in large part on the class, race, and age composition of the neighborhood (Manning, 1984, 1988).

- *Assumption 2.* The public is of one mind, a homogeneous populate whose satisfaction or dissatisfaction with the police can be readily measured.

The research in Seattle showed that different communities and neighborhoods had different expectations of the police and were not of one mind regarding the local police organization.

- *Assumption 3.* The police should be responsible for actively helping to define and shape community norms.

This assumption is closely related to the ideas espoused by several scholars during the 1980s regarding the utility of the police as agents of social control (Wilson and Kelling, 1982; Kelling, 1985, 1987; Sykes, 1986). Riechers and Roberg (1990) argue that police scholars are at odds with each other regarding the police on two counts. First is the lack of agreement regarding the proper role of police in a class-divided society; second is the disagreement regarding police as change agents in local communities. Manning (1984) suggests that there is a certain contentiousness in claiming that the police, having knowledge of the informal social control mechanism in a community, can possibly manipulate the community. He contends that the informal control mechanism of a community can be illegal and in conflict with the duty of the police to enforce legal norms.

- *Assumption 4.* Public fear stems more from disorder than from crime.

Brown and Wycoff (1987) found that African-American renters in Houston, Texas, were unaffected by attempts to reduce fear of personal victimization and crime. Recently, Skogan (1990) made similar comments regarding community policing and its applicability to diverse populations. For example, homeowners were more likely to have knowledge of community policing and were, therefore, more able to utilize programs and activities initiated by the police.

- *Assumption 5.* Signs of neglect and decay in neighborhoods invite crime.

Several criminologists have argued that the deterioration of neighborhoods makes them fertile ground for street crime. The "broken window" metaphor sounds good in theory, and several studies have attempted to ascertain the validity of this assumption. However, it would take longitudinal research to determine if the assumption is valid. The neighborhood would have to be observed both before and after signs of neglect and decay began to show.

- *Assumption 6.* Community policing programs begin with the initiative of the police with the aim of improving service, not of giving influential citizens control over police services.

A meticulous look at the community policing initiative in Seattle, however, showed that around 20 instrumental citizens influenced the development of community policing in Seattle.

- *Assumption 7.* Community policing can be done without violating the political neutrality of the police.

- *Assumption 8.* Police organizations, given their current mechanistic characteristics, can readily adapt to a more organic model required to effectively implement community policing.

- *Assumption 9.* Police organizations, given their current quality of personnel, can be responsive to the demands of community policing.

Assumptions 7 through 9, as articulated by policing scholars, focus on internal and external workings of police organizational dynamics.

These scholars question whether the police organizations are structured to adapt to the new changes as outlined by Trojanowicz (1990) and Goldstein (1993).

- *Assumption 10*. The police are the proper agency to fulfill the goals of community policing.

Community policing has been defined by some advocates as a solution to the crime problem. Assumption 10 presents a dilemma for both community policing and problem-solving policing in light of the literature reviewed. It stands to reason that a society which evidences racial and social cleavages would experience multitudinous problems in implementing a philosophy such as community policing.

These assumptions provide an overview of the underlying values traditionally associated with community policing in the United States. Research shows, however, that in some cases, the rhetoric of community policing proponents does not fit with the reality of what the police do (Klockars, 1988; Weatheritt, 1988). Several scholars have critiqued these assumptions and myths (Greene and Mastrofski, 1988; Robinson et al., 1994; Rosenbaum, 1994; Kappeler, 1995). The point of view of the scholars regarding the emergence of the community policing movement depends on whether they support the police or not.

Critiques of the Community Policing Movement

Critiques of the new policing gained momentum and shape after the 1988 publication of *Community Policing* by Greene and Mastrofski. The following provides an overview of the critiques of community policing and how they compare to Seattle's experience:

- The rhetoric of community policing's proponents will create expectations that are impossible to meet (Klockars, 1988; Manning, 1988).

Some citizen groups in Seattle associated the community policing small units with new and improved policing.

- The crime control mission of the police could get lost in the context of community policing's multiple goals (Bayley, 1988; Klockars, 1988; Hartmann et al., 1988).

Some segments of the Seattle community wanted prevention activities, not control-related tactics.

- Community organizing efforts of the police could produce nothing more than a political action group sustained and directed by the police themselves (Klockars, 1988; Bayley, 1988).

The 15-Point Plan in Seattle was indicative of an organizing effort instituted by the police department.

- The police could themselves be co-opted by the community and lose the will to maintain public order (Bayley, 1988).

In Seattle, the police and a small influential group were alleged to have co-opted the poor and powerless communities.

- The police could extend their reach undesirably far into the social and cultural life of the community (Bayley, 1988).

This type of influence happened in Seattle with police-school activities and programs.

- The interests of minorities in the neighborhoods could go unprotected by the police because of their desire to respond to the wishes of the majority (Bayley, 1988; Mastrofski, 1988; Manning, 1988; Williams and Murphy, 1990; Skogan, 1990).

Community policing in Seattle had multiple dimensions, as will be detailed in this research, that is, cooperation, co-optation, etc.

- The shift in supervisory responsibilities and styles required by community policing might not be made effectively, with a consequent increase in police corruption or abusive behavior (Bayley, 1988; Wasserman and Moore, 1988).

Community policing was piecemeal and evidenced no major changes in supervisory tactics or styles.

The comments noted above, although not exhaustive, provide a comprehensive overview of the critiques of the new community-oriented policing and problem-solving policing movement in the United

States. Presently, many police departments all over the country claim to be trying to solve the crime problem. Although community policing has been articulated as the answer and cure-all for gangs, guns, graffiti, riots, police brutality, and both public nuisance and street-level crime, it cannot be expected to solve all of the crime in all of the neighborhoods instantly. It will take a long-term commitment from the police and the neighborhood citizens.

THEORETICAL FRAMEWORKS

This study utilized three theories to analyze the politics of community policing in Seattle. These theories are important because they illuminate these politics in the context of Seattle and provide insight into the development, design, and implementation of Seattle's version of community policing. Legitimation processes, urban political processes, and micro-organizational processes were used as the basis for this case study of the politics of community policing in Seattle.

First, legitimation processes suggest that broader fiscal issues of the state are at work when one studies the crime control policies of contemporary cities (Harring, 1983). Second, urban political processes imply that complex interactions exist between public and private institutions, between the marketplace and the public sphere, and between private goals and collective purposes (Judd and Kantor, 1992). Third, micro-organizational processes propose that police departments, as traditional bureaucratic organizations, will adapt and change to deal with political pressure and, in some cases, will negotiate and implement minor reforms to appease constituencies.

Legitimation Processes

The concept of legitimacy is important to this case study because it helps explain how social arrangements are made to seem right or appropriate (Greenberg, 1981). Gurr (1970) remarks that regimes are said to be legitimate to the extent that their citizens regard them as proper and deserving of support. Given this general yardstick, urban policing has been experiencing a crisis of legitimacy since the 1960s (Harring, 1983). Confidence in the political efficacy of institutions like the police has been falling since the 1960s in many neighborhoods and communities (Reed, 1995). Police executives and administrators have been seeking a symbolic response to uncertainty and turbulence in the environment. Community policing provides a way of policing economic class divisions so as to avoid the serious public conflicts that have plagued police in recent years. Before the Rodney King debacle, many police departments wanted to be perceived as class neutral and supportive of all citizen anti-crime efforts.

Crime control and crime control policies of contemporary cities such as Seattle are presented with a major dilemma regarding how best to police inner city residents. For instance, the Federal Weed & Seed program was offered as a solution to street crime in large United States cities. Seattle was one of the first twenty cities to receive a federal grant for the implementation of a Weed & Seed program, which was touted as a bridge to developing community policing initiatives.

Some urban communities and/or neighborhoods tend to be fractured along lines of race, class, and gender, and come into contact with police and law enforcement officials daily. Urban police departments are faced with responding to calls for service and are ill-prepared to deal with deep-seated structural problems that plague urban communities.

Legitimation theory suggests that the helplessness of contemporary capitalism to reduce its contradictions presents the system with an ideological dilemma of vast proportions and that the management of this crisis becomes more and more a major activity of the bourgeoisie. Legitimation theory has been examined in such institutions as criminology, capitalism, and criminal justice administration (Greenberg, 1981; Brogden, 1982; Reiner, 1985; Wright, 1978; Katznelson, 1992; Harrigan, 1993; Michalowski, 1993). Beauregard (1993) contends that capitalists need legitimacy to exploit new frontiers. However, this researcher also contends that service is the agent of legitimation when scholars discuss the new community policing initiatives.

Urban Political Processes

The political economy of urban political processes implies that complex relationships exist between public entities, such as cities and private institutions. Among the marketplace and public sphere there also exists complicated relationships and processes. The public sphere is affected by governmental decision-making and actions made on behalf of the marketplace. The relationship between private goals and collective purposes is especially complicated and often misunderstood. Manning (1995:384) discusses how market economists and police experts forge community policing language. He states that community policing must be viewed as a competitive, service-producing activity that must show a profit and distribute services to its customers and/or clients. Therefore, community policing is viewed in terms of its economic impact on the community and police department.

Urban political processes theory explains events and factors such as racism, homelessness, and economic disparity, the latter which includes lack of money for vital city services. Also, political economy research assists scholars in understanding the enduring tensions between the haves and the have-nots played out at the grassroots level (Judd and Kantor, 1992).

Micro-Organizational Processes

Micro-organizational theory literature that highlights planned change and police culture helps one appreciate how the Seattle Police Department (SPD), a traditional bureaucratic organization, resisted change, adapted to change, negotiated change, and/or co-opted issues of crime control with neighborhood groups and community-based organizations. The micro-organizational theory literature has been applied to the police organization since the early 1960s (Bennis, Benne, and Chin, 1969; Toch, Grant, and Galvin, 1975; Brown, 1981; Lipsky, 1980).

Despite the varied definitions of community policing and theoretical perspectives previously discussed, this study enters the debate over community policing by examining one police department's efforts to implement a philosophy of citizen-police collaboration. The author contends that the development, design, and implementation of community policing is political and highly symbolic in nature. Furthermore, the author believes that community policing should be a process whereby police get out of their cars and take seriously those issues which are nominated by the citizens who are impacted by street crime. This goes along with the belief that community police officers should be "of and in" the community (Robinson et al., 1994:163). This research utilized a multi-theoretical framework to investigate and understand the development of community policing in Seattle, Washington during the years 1985-1993.

METHODOLOGY

The research in Seattle used multiple case study methodologies to link ideas and evidence. The ethnographic case study methodology was employed as a research strategy in the study of the Seattle Police Department and its relationship to two local high-crime areas of the city (the central district and the south end). However, this research will not cover every conflict, and will not examine many of the subtle nuances related to community policing in Seattle. This case study links the empirical and the theoretical and uses theory to make sense of evidence uncovered and to sharpen and refine the theories employed.

The interplay described above helps produce theoretically structured descriptions of the empirical world that are both useful and meaningful (Ragin and Becker, 1992). Scholars suggest that case studies have a twofold importance in studying social institutions. First, casing is an essential part of the process of understanding social phenomena. Cases are invoked to link ideas and evidence. Second, casing is an essential part of the process of producing theoretically structured descriptions of social life and of using empirical evidence to articulate theories (Ragin and Becker, 1992).

This author believes that a case is not inherently one thing or another, but rather a way station in the process of producing empirical social science. Furthermore, cases are multiple in most research efforts because ideas and evidence may be linked in many different ways.

Recent Community Policing Research

A recent example of a one-dimensional case study is research employed by Donald L. Yates (1993) to study community policing efforts in the Fort Worth (Texas) Police Department. He bases the entire study on a comprehensive report of community policing implementation in that police department. The paper examines the problems of implementing community policing in that department, and concludes that (1) some local departments are not in adequate possession of the goals and aims of community policing, and (2) that local departments have failed to prioritize community policing relative to traditional law enforcement strategies. On the other hand, a 1994 Ph.D. dissertation by Charles Moose at Portland State University was illuminating in understanding policing in the city of Portland, Oregon, and the delivery of social and medical services to low-income families residing in a housing project. His study was comprehensive and long-term (three years).

Several recent studies informed this research on community policing in Seattle. Notably, several authors have researched police departments utilizing multi-faceted approaches to understanding community policing (George, 1993; Lanier, 1993; Mastrofski, 1993). This research shows that investigators cannot rely solely on internal police research studies to make sense of a complex phenomenon such as community policing in a major metropolitan city.

In the following case study, over thirty interviews were conducted with local community leaders and crime-prevention groups in Seattle. Also, the chief and several police officials of various ranks were interviewed. Testimony before the Seattle City Council regarding the federal Weed & Seed program was taped and transcribed. In addition, newspaper accounts were gathered through the local public library and one of the major city papers (*Seattle Times*). Federal census data from 1990 and recent demographic information regarding the city of Seattle were also employed. Finally, official and unofficial community documents and other government documents were utilized to understand the politics of community policing in Seattle.

IMPORTANCE OF CASE STUDY

This case study is significant because the problems facing metropolitan Seattle are common to cities of similar size, population, and growth expansion. The theoretical framework is innovative and creative in understanding Seattle's political culture. Also, the multi-methodological approach is inventive and offers the reader a diversity of angles for understanding Seattle's urban growth and inner city decay.

This study links multi-theoretical approaches to the extensive methodological techniques utilized and links community policing growth and development to political processes. The interviews employed demonstrate the manifestation of crime control and prevention at the street level in Seattle. The interviews also illuminated the effects of external and internal pressures on the bureaucracy of the department. The newspapers (*Seattle Times* and *Seattle Post Intelligencer*) illustrate the publicness of crime and Seattle's political influence regarding community policing.

This study is important because it examines how one police department maneuvered through internal and external political pressures to create what has come to be defined as a model for community policing (Fleissner et al., 1992). These pressures are important to this study within the context and culture of Seattle. The pressures are unique to Seattle because of the influence that one small group had within the Seattle Police Department regarding the design and implementation of community policing. The knowledge to be gained from Seattle's experience is to refrain from letting one elitist, non-representative group dictate the public policy in the formation of community policing strategies. The police department gained legitimacy with the public and maintained organizational unity within the agency by overcoming obstacles and dealing effectively with pressures (Fleissner et al., 1992).

Internal Pressures

Although the Seattle Police Department evidenced a substantial increase in its budget in recent years, no new money was spent on community policing (Reed, 1995). The department resisted the development of a deadly force policy and withstood the pressures from local groups to implement such a policy. The police union was very powerful and opposed any reforms in the areas of deadly force and external oversight of departmental operations. Historically, the department showed a resistance to internal changes in its organizational structure (Scheingold, 1991). For example, no structural changes were made with the implementation of community policing. Although community policing proponents suggested that the organization should be flattened out to reap the benefits of the philosophy in practice, the management showed only a willingness to add on popular programs funded by the federal government (Scheingold, 1991). Community policing initiatives in Seattle will be described throughout this study as organizational add-ons to ongoing law enforcement.

A 1991 audit of the Seattle Police Department was performed by Carroll Buracher and Associates of Virginia. Among the recommendations suggested were increasing the number of officers in the department and institutionalizing community policing in all four precincts of the Seattle Police Department. Internally, the audit put pressure on the city to implement community policing and do something about street crime. Many new officers were aware of the emerging community policing movement nationwide and wanted to do different types of policing out on the streets. Many community policing advocates supported proactive deployment strategies that utilized hardware as well as software police technology. Both groups were aware that traditional policing was not helping them in the fight against emerging gangs, guns, and graffiti on their beats and in their neighborhoods.

External Pressures

The external pressures facing the Seattle Police Department from community-based groups and minorities were numerous during the years under study. For instance, the department reported the increased need for services (1988-1992 Annual Reports). The city witnessed an increase in street crimes, gangs, drug usage, and the availability of handguns. Other problems the city evidenced included the growth in unemployment, homelessness, and panhandlers, and an overcrowded jail downtown during the period of this research (1985-1993).

FUTURE OF SOCIAL ORGANIZATION AND COMMUNITY POLICING RESEARCH

The theoretical and policing implications of utilizing a multi-methodological and multi-theoretical framework are quite promising. These particular frameworks allow the researcher to observe and analyze complex political and economic pressures at work in contemporary cities such as Seattle.

For instance, in Houston, Texas, Skogan (1990) found that the benefits of community policing were largely reserved for white citizens and better-off residents of the target communities. The evaluations conducted by Skogan and his associates indicate that these groups had knowledge of the programs and participated in them, but that minorities and low-income residents did not. Skogan theorized that most of the desirable results of the program were confined to one segment of the community. Furthermore, the class bias could be traced to the way in which community policing activities were organized. He argued that it can be risky for the police to open themselves to input in communities that are diverse and to move beyond enforcing the criminal code. When police departments become involved in negotiating the character of local order, policing becomes an overtly political process.

This research extends the scope of previous community policing research and studies by looking at political processes and pressures between the years 1985-1993 in Seattle which propelled the department into implementing its version of community policing. The procedures that the Seattle Police Department followed serve as an example for

other cities of what to do and what not to do when designing and
implementing their own community policing program.

CHAPTER 2

Community Policing

ORIGINS OF COMMUNITY POLICING

Community policing has been described as the first major reform in policing since police departments embraced scientific management principles more than half a century ago (Trojanowicz and Bucqueroux, 1990). Generally speaking, United States policing has British roots. Sir Robert Peel is credited with influencing United States policing and the present community policing movement. Peel introduced the metropolitan police in 1829. These officers are famously known as "bobbies," a nickname honoring Sir Robert Peel.

Walker (1992) indicates that the London police introduced three new elements to modern policing. The first was a new mission to prevent crime. The second was a strategy of preventive patrol. The third was organizational structure. Peel borrowed the organizational structure of the London police from the military, including the uniforms, rank designations, and, most important, the authoritarian system of command and discipline. Walker suggests that this quasi-military style prevails in American police administration to this day.

Bayley (1985) states that the essential features of the modern police are that they are public, specialized, and professional. They are public in the sense that they transfer responsibility for public safety to government agencies. They are specialized in the sense that they have a distinct mission of law enforcement and crime prevention. Finally, they are professional in the sense that they are full-time, paid employees.

There is a large and growing body of literature on the community policing movement. The growth of this literature began in the 1980s, and exploded with the publication of Greene and Mastrofski's anthology, *Community Policing: Rhetoric or Reality* (1988). There are numerous books on the subject (Skolnick and Bayley, 1986; Goldstein, 1990; Sparrow, Moore, and Kennedy, 1990; Trojanowicz and Bucqueroux, 1990; Toch and Grant, 1991; McElroy, Cosgrove, and Sadd, 1993; Kappeler, Sluder, and Alpert, 1994; Robinson, Scaglion, and Olivero, 1994; Kappeler, 1995). Police executives have also written extensively on this subject (Brown, 1985, 1989; Couper and Lobitz, 1991; Stamper, 1994). Most recently, Rosenbaum (1994) contended that community policing has been spawned by major police executive organizations, by the federal government, and by Presidents Bush and Clinton's public commitment to fight crime and rebuild cities. Also, Eck and Rosenbaum (1994) report that community policing is part of a larger set of changes in progress throughout the United States. For example, many of the management practices used by community policing advocates (e.g., decentralizing decision-making, problem-solving teams, attention to customer needs, and others) are used widely in industry. They cite racial fairness and quality of life issues as major themes in community policing, and indicate that it is only one manifestation of social concerns and awareness.

The literature on community policing has gained increased notoriety in law enforcement and academic circles, as reflected in the number of publications and police departments reporting the initiation of community policing programs (Goldstein, 1993). The community policing movement has created controversy and acrimony, with a division into two camps: community policing advocates and community policing opponents.

Community Policing Advocates

Community policing advocates are a diverse lot of law enforcement officials, academicians, and community development leaders. They perceive the community as an agent and partner in promoting security rather than as a passive audience (Sparrow, 1988). Reducing crime is the explicit objective of law enforcement agencies. Using the techniques associated with reducing crime, this is achieved by reducing disorder and fear of crime, in part by creating a sense of cohesion among law-abiding citizens (Goldstein, 1990).

The concept of community policing envisages a police department striving for an absence of crime and disorder. Community policing advocates see police primarily in the multiple roles of offering assistance, mediating disputes, maintaining community order, as well as providing public safety (Trojanowicz, 1990). Ideally, community policing is not a particular program within a department, but instead should be the dominant philosophy throughout the department (Brown, 1989). Some advocates question the rising popularity of community policing and indicate that it might further improve the relationship between the police and minorities (Williams and Murphy, 1990). The latter authors question whether poor and/or minority communities are empowered enough to reap the benefits of community policing. However, community policing has its cheerleaders. Trojanowicz (1991) even goes so far as to say that community policing curbs police brutality. Also, Trojanowicz and Bucqueroux (1992) say that community policing reform should reinvent the old-fashioned beat cop as today's community officer. They said that he would then act as a neighborhood organizer and problem solver rather than just as a visible deterrent to crime.

Community Policing Opponents

Community policing opponents are also a diverse lot, consisting of academicians, some police departments, rank-and-file officers, some middle managers, and social critics. Klockars (1988) argues that community policing is currently more rhetoric than reality. Miles (1992), one of the foremost opponents of community policing, indicates that it amounts to a steady, low-level involvement by a residential force with the law-abiding portion of the population in an effort to control the law-breaking portion of the population. Another opponent suggests that community policing could lead to inequitable or illegal policing (Wycoff, 1988). A long-time police scholar comments that community policing could lead to weakened community ties and further dependence on the police (Manning, 1988). Another police scholar indicates that community policing is one of the latest in a fairly long tradition of circumlocutions, the purpose of which is to conceal, mystify, and legitimate police force (Klockars, 1988).

Some scholars suggest that community policing must be supported by police management in order to work properly. Community policing, as practiced by police agencies, is mostly a pipe dream (Reichers and Roberg, 1990). An international scholar of policing suggests that community policing represents an increasingly important aspect of policing the inner city crisis and the political nature of policing (Gordon, 1987).

The political nature of community policing has been discussed in detail by European scholars. The very concept of effective community policing was never explained adequately, or defined, by the police departments aiming for its implementation (Cashmore, 1991).

One of the strongest contentions about community policing comes from a scholar and administrator in New York state government whom the researcher interviewed. He wanted to know what the mechanisms are for the implementation of community policing. He vehemently suggested that no formal mechanism exists to implement the philosophy or practice called community policing (Christianson, 1993).

The quest for a return to the good old days of bobbies patrolling the streets is at the core of the community policing movement. However, the community policing movement has sought to built support for the police organization among low-income and underclass citizens. When one is referring to community-police relations, the concern is not with all communities. Few, if any, advocates are troubled by community-police relations in upper-class or upper-middle-class communities. The focus is often on neighborhoods that consist of the poor, minorities, female-headed households, and young unemployed adults (Robinson et al., 1994). In a 20-year review of community policing programs, Trojanowicz et al. (1986) found that community policing programs targeted minority, low-income, and high-crime communities. They cite a crime-prevention project in Atlanta, Georgia; a foot patrol project in a low-income area in Fort Worth, Texas; a crime deterrent program in Los Angeles aimed at blacks and Hispanics; a ride-along program in an area that is 95 percent black and poor in Menlo Park, California; a program to improve attitudes about police in a densely populated African-American community in Miami; and finally, a concerned citizens action hotline to enlist African-American support in Youngstown, Ohio.

COMMUNITY POLICING LITERATURE

The community policing literature has been dominated by several sources. First, Michigan State University's National Center on Community Policing produces a newsletter, *Foot Prints*, which explores contemporary issues in community-oriented policing. The Winter 1990 issue focused on neighborhood network centers and the expansion of the community policing model. The Fall/Winter 1992 issue, from the Director's Corner, focused on the basics of community policing. Second, the United States Department of Justice, the National Institute of Justice, and the program in criminal justice policy and management at the John F. Kennedy School of Government, Harvard University, have an extensive series entitled "Perspectives on Policing." Numerous law enforcement officials and scholars have written papers on community policing since the mid-1980s. Third, the National Institute of Justice has published several articles on community policing in the last couple of years. Specifically, in August 1992, the Department of Justice programs published several important articles about Seattle, including "Community Policing in Seattle: A Model Partnership between Citizens and Police" by Fleissner, Fedan, Stotland, and Klinger (1992).

Goldstein (1990), in particular, has influenced a number of community policing programs worldwide. For instance, he took part in some early experiments involving problem-oriented policing in Madison, Wisconsin; Baltimore County, Maryland; with the London Metropolitan Police; in Newport News, Virginia; and with the Seattle Police Department. Goldstein discusses the results of these experiments in his 1990 publication, *Problem-Oriented Policing*. He is widely recognized for helping the public understand that police must move beyond just handling incidents of crime, and instead get out of the patrol cars and solve problems of concern to community residents.

Rosenbaum (1994) gathered and organized one of the most comprehensive group of writings on community policing and problem-solving policing. This edited work is important because it presents and discusses community policing theory and philosophy for the first time in one volume. Also, Rosenbaum's volume introduces multi-site assessments, community policing and agency implementation, community policing's impact on community residents and neighborhood problems, community policing in Canada and Great Britain, community policing issues and concerns, and finally, an elaborate research synthesis with policy ramifications.

COMMUNITY POLICING IN SEATTLE

A brief overview of community policing in Seattle will set the stage for a more intensive examination in the following chapters. In a 1994 article, Carter and Radelet suggest that the ingredients necessary for community policing to work both philosophically and programmatically include mission statement changes, decentralization of the organization, problem-solving mechanisms, public involvement, change in police attitude toward citizens, performance evaluation rewards, in-service training for new recruits, and permanent beat boundaries.

None of the above existed in Seattle, and public involvement was also limited. There were police-community liaisons in every precinct, but the activities were directed by the police. The bottom line is that it was not community policing as espoused by scholars. Therefore, in Seattle during the period of 1985-1993, the mayor's office and the police department, in consultation with the South Seattle Crime Prevention Council (SSCPC), fashioned a variant form of community policing. The extensive purpose of this new program was to do something about crime in two target neighborhoods known for gun violence and street crimes. This was a bastardized version of the philosophy of true community policing. The police department developed and maintained an ongoing relationship with the SSCPC. This was an elitist group; the meetings were by invitation only, and the regular meetings were not widely publicized. The outgrowth of these meetings led to the development of community policing teams. The main purpose of the teams was to focus on crimes that contributed to physical and social disorder and neighborhood decay (Fleissner et al., 1992). The characteristics of community policing politics in Seattle were: (1) no organizational changes were made in the police department hierarchy, (2) the police department and the mayor's office accepted the 15-Point Plan, which was crafted by the SSCPC in the high-crime area, (3) there was no change in the mission statement of the police department, and (4) there was limited community involvement by residents in the target districts.

Meaning of Community Policing in Seattle

In reality, the Seattle Police Department implemented a form of community policing teams based on specialty units in four precincts citywide. No real commitment to the goals and philosophy of community policing outlined above was evident during the author's two visits to Seattle in the summer of 1993. One officer who headed the six-member community policing team in the East Precinct was interviewed. He indicated that community policing meant freeing officers from 911 calls and the isolation of their patrol cars and the ability to re-establish face-to-face relationships with community residents and prevent crimes rather than react when they happen. This officer seemed to be taking the weight off the East Precinct and placing it on the shoulders of his small unit. Thus, for him, it was largely a matter of improving police working conditions.

This unit faced enormous pressures from the rank-and-file officers. The researcher learned that rank-and-file officers were jealous of the specialty units and considered the work of the community policing officers to be social work, not police work. For the most part, his unit's duties were attending block watch and crime-prevention meetings, and performing intercessions to get a pile of garbage cleaned up, a broken street light replaced, or a negligent landlord to look after his or her property.

There was no department-wide commitment to the public relations policing activities evidenced by the sergeant and his unit. The author was able to confirm this observation with several high-ranking Seattle Police Department officials and community residents. The community leaders interviewed seemed to appreciate the small community policing teams; however, they felt that no commitment existed at the top echelons of city government or with the police chief for genuine expansion of community policing department-wide. Most important, several residents in the high crime district felt limited support for the eradication of street-level drug sales, prostitution, and sporadic gun violence.

Top-Down Policing in Seattle

Skolnick and Bayley (1986) intimate that community policing is not soft on crime, that traditional law enforcement duties continue, and that other responsibilities are in addition to, rather than a substitute for, community policing. They imply that community policing is not a specialized unit or group and that the concept works well when every member of the bureau is involved, trained, and committed to the philosophy of community policing. Finally, community policing is not a top-down approach, because the full-blown philosophy or concept actively seeks input from all involved officers and administrators. ("Top-down" policing is a traditional approach in which the police set the public safety agenda and are the experts regarding crime prevention and control.)

This author's research, on the other hand, demonstrates that community policing in Seattle was still classical top-down policing with a heavy emphasis on police-community relations. The department developed a strategy for the local community and was the "expert" on crime control and crime prevention activities in consultation with the South Seattle Crime Prevention Council.

Crime Control Versus Crime Prevention

Community policing in Seattle was largely a crime control program with the express purpose of improving the relationship between inner city residents and the Seattle Police Department. Evidence gathered suggests that the department used the SSCPC, a.k.a. Rainier Chamber of Commerce, to help set targets and public policy (Fleissner et al., 1991). Specifically, Fleissner et al. (1991:71) indicate that one of the most unique forms of collaboration between the SSCPC and the Seattle Police Department was the program of setting targets. They state:

> The initial, informal approach to targeting was introduced at the first meeting called by the SSCPC on December 30, 1987, just prior to the formal start of the program. Invitations to this meeting were sent to core members of the SSCPC and other selected community organizations. . . . it was the consensus that the targets were to be formally designated at meetings of the SSCPC; that is, the decision as to where police were to concentrate their efforts was to be made at an official meeting of a community organization with no formal governmental status, a truly radical step in American policing.

On the surface, this seems to be an ideal relationship based on collaboration and partnership. However, at close examination, approximately seventeen people influenced the police department into believing that they truly represented the majority of the people in South Seattle. The best thing that could be said about this group is that they were resource-rich and well-organized. They were involved in other activities to help the police department and supported their vested interests. For example, they developed narcotic activity reports, criminal trespass programs, pay telephone programs, drug trafficking civil abatement programs, anti-graffiti programs, the telephone hotline, and the garden police car program.

Critics of the department indicated that the community policing program should have been extended department-wide. Interviews conducted by the researcher revealed community leaders and residents describing community policing in Seattle as a crime *control* strategy and police leaders describing it as a crime *prevention* strategy. The researcher found that the south end residents, lead by the SSCPC, wanted to come down on street criminals and gain department support for those activities. However, in the central district, disorganized African-American leaders were unable to gain support for their crime-prevention activities. One explanation for this could be that they were critical of the police department's actions on the streets of the central district. Residents in the central district wanted good policing, not heavy-handed law enforcement. One scholar has documented that the politicization of crime differed in the central district from the south end and that the political culture was also different (Scheingold, 1991).

Community policing in Seattle was the result of the politics of one neighborhood group and the police department attempting to do something about crime in the southeast part of town. Was this traditional policing, or community policing with a new friendly face? The researcher contends that this model outlined by its proponents was basically traditional policing with organizational add-ons where no structural changes were evidenced. Examples of add-ons are the Mountain Bike Patrol program, Community Police Teams, the Gang Unit, Anti-crime teams, Seattle Teen for Youth, Weed & Seed, and Residential and Business Watch.

The police department continued to do business as usual and accepted praise for the model. The Seattle Police Department merged community policing and traditional policing. For instance, the department continued to arrest street dealers for illegal drug sales, to crack down on gang activity, to police prostitution and noise disturbances, and to police trespassing, loitering, and graffiti artists and abandoned vehicles on the streets of Seattle. The Seattle Police Department made no changes in its mission statement, in increasing public involvement in policing, or in its attitude or outreach toward marginalized citizens. In contrast, the Portland (Oregon) Police Bureau made enormous inroads in involving the public in community policing programs and partnerships. The Portland Police Bureau also hosted the first international conference on community policing (Portland Police Bureau Community Policing Strategic Plan, 1994).

On the surface, the Seattle Police Department seemed to develop a problem-solving technology. It attempted to resolve some of the problems evidenced in neighborhoods that needed police services the most. The criteria seemed to be organization and support of the police agenda. This research shows that the department went into this token form of community policing kicking and screaming. However, the department gained local and national publicity for the community policing variation.

One example of the internal problems in the department was complaint resolution. A 1992 study by the Seattle Police Department Planning Section indicated that only one-third of people wanting to file a complaint actually did so. However, Bereano, a member of the police-citizen committee, alleged that only 50 percent of those filing were satisfied with how the complaint was actually handled, that is, a satisfaction rate of only one-sixth of the people with grievances (Fleissner et al., 1992). However, the results of the police study are defended by a report issued during the summer of 1993 by a former municipal judge (Terrence Carroll) handling internal complaints in the Seattle Police Department.

Overall, the police chief and department developed a proactive response to menacing problems facing some communities. For example, the patrol division, located in the operations bureau of the police department, was involved in a range of reactive activities, such as responding to domestic violence incidents, crimes in progress, civil complaints, and referral to community services. Traditional policing activities, such as preventive patrol, demonstration management, dignitary protection, and other unusual occurrences seemed to work well department-wide. For instance, the department managed the 1990 Goodwill Games for over two weeks without reported major incidents.

Observations lead this researcher to surmise that community policing in Seattle was subtly constructed to gain and maintain legitimacy with all classes in the city. Specifically, the purpose of the program seemed to be twofold: to bring the lower class and marginalized citizens into supporting policing activities; and to accept the tactics suggested by the police to do something about the street crime problem. Consequently, community policing seeks legitimacy and consent and co-opts powerless citizens accepting into police agendas. Selznick (1949) indicates that co-optation is a process of absorbing new elements into the leadership or policy-determining structure of an organization as a means of averting threats to its stability or existence.

Differences in Community Policing in Seattle

Community policing in Seattle differs from other models because of the city's particular political culture and its governmental structure. Seattle has a nine-member city council and, most recently, a consensus-building city hall. Most important, Seattle had a chief of police who had been in office for 15 years, while the national average is about three-and-a-half years. He took control of a department, cleaned up the corruption, and was able to maintain an amiable relationship with the press. Evidence reveals that he had conflictual relationships with some vocal community leaders, which may have resulted in the us versus them mentality within the police organization. This mentality was exacerbated by the fact that many police officers lived outside of the Seattle city limits. One of the cornerstones of true community policing is to have police reside in the area they police.

The political structure of Seattle's government could best be described as liberal and progressive regarding social issues, and the people attracted to city government believed themselves to be thus. However, old-timers described the city as conservative. Another feature of the city is a plethora of neighborhood groups and community-based organizations. For instance, one of the city's neighborhood directors indicated that Seattle has over 100 organized neighborhood groups, which meet monthly around the city and discuss issues facing their respective communities. This process can best be described as interest group liberalism (Lowi, 1969).

Internal and External Pressures

Numerous internal and external pressures were placed on the Seattle Police Department during the period under study to do something about the street crime problem in the south end and the central district of the city. The three theories utilized in this study (legitimation processes, urban political processes, and micro-organizational processes) helped the researcher understand both internal and external pressures. *Internal pressures* were the city budget, allegations of police brutality, deadly force policy, consultant and internal audits, deployment strategies, and small community policing teams. *External pressures* were an increase in gangs, drugs, and guns; drive-by shootings; unemployment;

homelessness; panhandlers downtown; an increase in the number of skinheads; overcrowded jails; and increases in race, class, and ethnic conflicts.

The politics of community policing in Seattle were evidenced by social control mechanisms and public relations activities implemented to co-opt local community leaders, neighborhood organizations, indigenous organizations, business leaders, and police officers into police-driven crime prevention strategies that have limited community support and involvement.

CHAPTER 3

Legitimation Processes

Community policing in Seattle involves both social control mechanisms and public relations activities implemented to draw local community leaders, neighborhood organizations, business leaders, and police officers into police-driven crime-prevention strategies that have limited community support and involvement. This research demonstrates that the politics of community policing are ideological and that the Seattle Police Department sought to maintain subtle consent and legitimacy from the local populace. Community policing is an ideological construct to maintain social control and support in a postmodern society filled with social ills and major fiscal problems.

This level of analysis focuses on legitimation processes. It suggests that the inability of contemporary capitalism to reduce its contradictions presents the political and economic system with an ideological dilemma of vast proportions. Beauregard (1993) contends that capitalists need legitimacy to exploit new frontiers. The management of this crisis becomes more and more a major activity of the organizational elites in society. Legitimation theory has been used by a number of scholars studying the relationship between crime, capitalism, and criminal justice administration to explain apparently contradictory actions on the part of governments (Wright, 1978; Greenberg, 1981; Brogden, 1982; Reiner, 1985; Katznelson, 1992; Harrigan, 1993; Michalowski, 1993).

Legitimation is the process by which social arrangements are made to seem right or appropriate, and it is regarded as more effective than force in maintaining dominant and exploitative relationships (Greenberg, 1981). Moulakis (1985:2) states, "Legitimacy is the regard in which a polity is held by its members and the extent to which that polity is thought to be worthy of support." Legitimacy can be lost, adapted, distorted, or maintained. One of the key mechanisms for maintaining the legitimacy in modern states is adherence to the rule of law (Thompson, 1975:258).

The concept of legitimacy is important because it explains how political, economic, and social arrangements are made to seem appropriate in civil society (Greenberg, 1981). Gurr (1970) states that regimes are said to be legitimate to the extent that their citizens regard them as proper and deserving of support.

Given this general yardstick, urban policing has been experiencing a crisis of legitimacy since the 1960s. Confidence in the political efficacy of institutions like the police has been falling since the 1960s in many low-income and high-crime neighborhoods and communities. Police executives and government administrators have been seeking a stronger proactive response to uncertainty and turbulence in downtown areas and in the inner city since the mid-1980s. Legitimation process theory helps articulate problems of confidence, trust, and belief in political systems and actors.

Brogden (1982:214) notes that community policing has developed sequentially out of service work. He notes, "Add juvenile to school liaison, organize a youth club or tenant's association, throw into the brew a dash of the Reithian leadership ethic, and the result is community policing." He asserts that within the broad rubric of the title (community policing), two general forms of police work can be distinguished—community involvement schemes and race relations work.

This chapter details what happened as the Seattle Police Department implemented the Community Outreach and Youth Appreciation Week in April, 1993. In all of its guises, community policing involves two general types of police work: *race relations work* and *community involvement schemes*. The outreach effort concerned the reconstruction of consent and legitimacy for the police department. The ostensible purpose of the project was to offset the possibility of a riot in Seattle following the anticipated Rodney King verdict in Los Angeles. Two relevant questions that guide this chapter will be answered: To what extent was the Seattle Police Department's public education program in the central district and south end neighborhoods concerned with legitimizing Seattle's version of community policing? And, did the Seattle Police Department suffer any threats or loss of its legitimacy in the eyes of the public in general or with specific segments of the city, including African-American, multi-racial, and low-income communities? The real story was the "tale of two communities." It was a tale of social class, with racial and political implications, in the south end and central district of Seattle.

COMMUNITY OUTREACH AND YOUTH APPRECIATION WEEK

The Seattle Police Department's closure report for South Community Police Team Project 93-1 (Community Outreach and Youth Appreciation Week) revealed the department's concern with legitimating Seattle's version of community policing. The report, dated April 27, 1993, was an internal memo from a sergeant (South Precinct Community Police Team) to the precinct lieutenant (operations commander of the South Precinct). This internal memo was important because it cut to the heart of the legitimation process in Seattle as the police department went about gaining support for DARE (Drug Abuse Resistance Education)-type activities in the south end.

Recent research shows that D.A.R.E. programs are a form of symbolic politics supported by direct and indirect stakeholders and embedded in a complex potent organizational support system (Wysong et al., 1994). Extensive research shows that the department and public officials extended themselves in an unusual manner by implementing this costly program. On the other hand, the department went into the token community policing program and failed to spend any funds for the implementation of community policing in Seattle (Fleissner et al., 1991).

As the story unfolds, it is worth mentioning that the Seattle Police Department's South Precinct (south end) is directly across the street from the Holly Park housing project, one of the largest public housing projects in the city of Seattle. It is home to over 1,000 residents and is considered a high-crime area by the Seattle Police Department (see Annual Reports 1985-1993).

Sergeant W.C. starts the memo (April 27, 1993) by stating:

It is safe to say that citizens have done a remarkable job of accepting citizen crime prevention and partnership with their local police agencies as holding the only hope for reducing crime and fear and making neighborhoods safer. In South Seattle, where this community policing team project began, the groups of citizens are already nationally acclaimed for their ability to organize and work with their police department in equal and trusting partnership. . . .The environment produced the working relationship that began community policing in 1990. As a result, a team of officers in the South precinct have had the opportunity to interact with the community very closely over the last 3 years. Relationships of respect and trust have been formed and maintained diligently by all concerned. This all occurred with the strong and personal support of the chief of police who has consistently encouraged and praised new initiatives and ideas born out of the interaction with the community. (p. 1)

The above-mentioned sergeant stated that in February 1993:

The minds of most police agencies in the United States were on the upcoming trial in Los Angeles and the potential for civil disorder. In discussing that issue and the problems we experienced last year downtown, I came to the conclusion that we in policing all too frequently concentrate on and prepare for the negative. It was very apparent that the 500 youth who were acting out downtown (Seattle) last year were not representative of the 59,000 youth who were not involved. (p. 1)

The sergeant devised a plan "for positive recognition and support for the responsible young people who did not conduct themselves that way" (memo, April 27, 1993). The purpose of the Community Outreach and Youth Appreciation Week was to gain legitimacy for the police organization, gather intelligence, and keep citizens' minds off what was going on in Los Angeles during the spring of 1993. The Seattle Police Department and government officials did not want to experience the same destruction of private property and lives as Los Angeles did after the first Rodney King verdict in 1992.

Community policing, as defined and articulated, is proactive and subtly ideological. Community policing scholars state:

"Blue uniform" policing or state police work implies a range of functions, namely enforcing (and sometimes defining) the criminal law, maintaining order, intelligence gathering, and securing consent, all directed towards a singular end: upholding the general legal framework of the state—by persuasion if possible, violently if necessary (Brogden et al., 1988:2).

The idea of the Community Outreach and Youth Appreciation Week was discussed with the South Precinct operations lieutenant, and the entire department initiated the project/mission during the first week of February 1993. According to the sergeant, "The goal of the project was to have extensive outreach and interaction with the citizens of the South Precinct, particularly the youth, and to provide them with some positive feedback, fun, and healthy activities during break" (Internal memo, April 27, 1993). He implied that it was best that the youth of the south end be kept busy during spring break of 1993.

The sergeant was involved in a subtle form of moral entrepreneurship (Gusfield, 1963). He felt he was doing "the right thing" by initiating this worthwhile project. His project/mission as planned was noble and sincere. However, when the politicians and police officials became involved, the whole process became a public relations ploy for legitimization and support led by SSCPC members and associates. This is apparent by names and high-profile leaders that were prominently involved in the Community Outreach and Youth Appreciation Week.

The sergeant acknowledged that it was "not politically popular to admit such, the timing of this effort also coincided with the possibility of the Rodney King verdict being reached during spring vacation." Specifically, he claimed, "This accentuated the need for extensive effort to go into the high schools and middle schools to 'educate' and allow the youth to vent anger and frustration" (Internal memo, April 27, 1993). Sergeant W.C. never fully explained or discussed the reasons why he believed that the youths in the south end middle and high schools might exhibit anger and frustration after the second Rodney King verdict. However, he gained extensive support from his superiors for the "noble" Community Outreach and Youth Appreciation Week proposal. The program was designed for subtle social control of the local community and neighborhoods, not to address underlying political-economic causes of the frustration.

Organization of the Project

The sergeant related that "the operation" gained fruition on February 16, 1993, with a joint planning session between the South Precinct Community Police Team and the Crime Prevention Unit of the Seattle Police Department. It is important to note that the Crime Prevention Unit, a civilian unit of the Seattle Police Department, had been operating for twenty years and was held in high esteem by local law-abiding citizens and politicians. For that reason, the project/mission had instant legitimacy and enormous support. After the meeting, both sets of actors agreed that the mission would have five components:

- Mayor's proclamation of "Youth Appreciation Week"
- Creation of Youth Outreach Teams for schools
- Community outreach in neighborhoods
- Facilitation of youth activity planning
- Strengthening of overall community-police partnership

All five components are important in understanding the project/mission in the Seattle public schools and local community. Sergeant W.C. claimed, "Our overall goal was to conduct a community outreach that would strengthen our bond with our community and to act as a catalyst and to provide positive youth activities during Youth Appreciation Week" (Internal memo, April 27, 1993).

The operation action report provided an in-depth description of each component. The South Precinct operations lieutenant approved of this plan, according to Sergeant W.C. The staff then met with the patrol division commander, who also approved of the operation, requesting only that they be provided with a list of community leaders who might be willing to assist in the event of civil disturbances.

The latter request is very important in understanding the version of community policing and the legitimation process of constructing it. Sergeant W.C. and his line staff determined that the south and east precincts would run separate programs based on the needs of each precinct. As the operation unfolded, the patrol division commander was requested to brief the mayor's staff on the mission and find out if the mayor would issue a proclamation declaring the week of April 5 through April 9, 1993, as Youth Appreciation Week.

According to the sergeant, the next step was a meeting between his office staff and Janice Corbin of the Crime Prevention Unit. "She was briefed on the project and asked to become a full partner," reported Sergeant W.C. Ms. Corbin accepted her role and began immediately suggesting "unique ideas and improvements," according to the memo. As plans unfolded, "within a week, the community policing team and Crime Prevention Unit had a joint meeting for all staff, and the planning and delegation of work was underway."

The sergeant said that one of the first priorities was to get the community involved as soon as possible. It should be noted that these were police-initiated activities, not community-initiated ones, thus the urgent need to get the community leaders on board. Consequently, the precinct decided to have a large community meeting on February 27, at 11:00 a.m., at Franklin High School (which is located on a major street, at an intersection between the central district and the south end). He reported, "All nine community policing team officers and all crime-prevention staff went to work, personally contacting as many community leaders as possible and asking them to come to the planning meeting" (Internal memo, April 27, 1993).

The South Precinct Community Police Team and the downtown crime-prevention staff (approximately 15 to 20 individuals) started intensive promotions regarding Youth Appreciation Week. Sergeant W.C. said that a follow-up letter was written by the Crime Prevention Unit and sent to over one hundred citizens who had already been personally contacted. The South Precinct Community Police Team made arrangements for the schoolrooms, direction signs, and refreshments for the leaders and other invitees.

The mayor and city council members liked the idea of Community Outreach and Youth Appreciation Week, and the mayor said he would sign a proclamation. The South Precinct Community Police Team prepared the proclamation for the mayor's signature and delivered it to his office. The proclamation was fine-tuned by the mayor's staff and signed. Moreover, Andrew Lofton of the mayor's office indicated that he would attend the meeting and bring the original signed proclamation.

The community meeting was held on February 27, 1993, and was attended by 62 community leaders from throughout the south end community (South Precinct area). Sergeant W.C. (Internal memo, April 27, 1993) reported:

> These were instrumental people in the community and were excited about the project. Lieutenant Sylve hosted the conference and Operations Bureau Command Staff made some comments to the audience. Sergeant Conn explained the project. The audience broke up into three separate groups based on South Seattle geographical boundaries. West Seattle...Beacon Hill and Georgetown...Rainier Valley. Each of the two community policing team officers from the

> area and a Group Facilitator from Crime Prevention. Their job was
> formulating plans for youth activities during spring break. (p. 3)

He indicated that the planning sessions went on for about an hour and
then follow-up meetings were scheduled for all three groups.

The group, under the leadership of Sergeant W.C., had achieved its
first goal to organize the community and gain support from the mayor's
office. They had the mayor's proclamation in hand. Sergeant W.C.
(Internal memo, April 27, 1993) explained:

> The second goal was to CREATE A YOUTH OUTREACH TEAM
> FOR THE SCHOOLS. The sergeant addressed the roll calls in the
> South Precinct and explained what we were trying to do with this
> project. Officer Darryl Williams heard the presentation and came
> forward after roll call and indicated he liked the idea and would be
> willing to help put together a team of officers from patrol to assist
> community policing team officers on the school portion of the project.
> They would go with community policing teams into the South Precinct
> high schools and middle schools to discuss Rodney King, Civil Rights
> Laws, the last Rodney King trial, and other matters of interest to the
> students. The Precinct Captain was asked to approve assigning four
> additional officers to this project for about three weeks prior to spring
> break. The four-officer team would be responsible for scheduling the
> schools so that we could talk with all the students at all six high
> schools and all five middle schools. Sergeant Conn set up a meeting
> with the principals of the south end middle schools and high schools.
> Captain Ferguson and Lieutenants Sylve and Conn then explained the
> program and requested the approval and support of the School
> administrations to present this education program. (p. 4)

The education of the south end community was in full swing. The
community policing teams and the crime-prevention staff were
organized and supportive of Youth Appreciation Week. The precinct
captains were on board. Community groups were involved, and Officer
Darryl Williams was supportive. The memo showed that Officer Darryl
Williams is African-American, and he felt his involvement was
important in this multi-racial effort for police-community relations.
Additionally, Sergeant W.C. wrote:

During this time Lieutenant Sylve contacted the U.S. Attorney's Office. They agreed to commit to an extensive two-week educational program. This would consist of going into the classroom with the community policing team officers in all the high schools to educate and lend credence to the program. We contacted Training and got video copies of the complete Rodney King Trial and a Ted Kopple special on the riots (Anatomy of a Riot). These tapes were shown to all officers who were going to be involved in this youth education project. In addition, Sally Gustafson from the U.S. Attorney's Office came to the South Precinct and underwent an extensive question and answer period on Civil Rights Law and the current trial in Los Angeles. This was videotaped by Training and then shown to all the officers who were going to be involved in the school education project. (p. 4)

The organization of the project required gathering all the relevant law enforcement actors and South Precinct officials to implement the Community Outreach and Youth Appreciation Week.

Implementation of the Project

The next phase of the project was to expedite the community outreach into the neighborhoods of the south end. Brogden (1982) defines these types of forums, or programs, as community involvement schemes used to gain and maintain consent and legitimacy in neighborhoods and in the larger community.

According to the memo, this portion of the project/mission required massive preparation exclusive of the other four parts. Specifically, the nine community police team officers were requested each to pick a high-crime-rate area in their district that had a high density of at-risk youth. The districts selected were to have geographical boundaries of roughly ten square blocks. The community policing team officers were then requested to prepare maps of the area. One officer prepared flyers for each of the areas to be surveyed so that they could be handed out in advance. The memo indicated that Officer R.E. "prepared a survey questionnaire and a second form to be left with residents so that they could mail in future problems or complaints."

The captain approved three patrol officers to work on the door-to-door outreach for the nine days during which the project was scheduled. The planning units organized every aspect of the operation. For instance, they made arrangements to have the mobile precinct van available on each of the nine days. Furthermore, they requested mounted patrol for the days they were in garden communities (the new name for public housing). In Holly Park and High Point public housing, translators were made available so that community policing team officers could include large numbers of Southeast Asians in the opinion surveys. Historically, the latter group had been omitted from Seattle Police Department opinion surveys and polls.

The unstated goal of this portion of the project was to gather intelligence data. Sergeant W.C. wrote that the project's secondary goal was to gather police and crime-related information. This point is very important, for it is an example of the goal of public relations policing that has been discussed previously. Brogden et al. (1988) indicate that police learned to turn a blind eye to certain infractions in the interest of the greater good of maintaining order or community acceptance. They defined the latter as the delicate art of negotiated or community policing of low-income and racially diverse neighborhoods. Community acceptance, subtly or overtly, is the basis for the production of community policing schemes and programs.

The stated goal of the project was to provide positive interpersonal exchange between citizens and their police officers in these volatile areas. However, the sergeant admitted, "There was a variety of information passed on to the police during the survey." He indicated that the information was either acted on or forwarded to other units. The horse patrol was a big attraction in the garden communities. "After the mounted patrol left the area, citizens both young and old came down to the mobile precinct to visit and see the horses they heard were in the area," reported the sergeant. The point of discussing the horse patrol is to illustrate that community policing-related activities are symbolic public relations tactics.

Police Public Relations

The sergeant reported that the community policing team officers from all three watches, crime-prevention officers, and a member of the C.S.O. team (community service officers) went door-to-door in the neighborhoods for nine consecutive working days. The public relations policing aspect of this mission was enormous and extremely rewarding, declared Sergeant W.C. For example, the police had positive contact with over 4,000 citizens during this outreach effort in the high-crime areas.

The research shows that community policing is purportedly concerned with police job satisfaction. Community policing officers develop "ownership" of the geographical area to which they are assigned over a long period of time. The community also develops a sense of "ownership" of the police officer as a friend and confidant. Therefore, the officer is respected by a citizen and seen as "my officer." Robinson et al. (1994:142) report, "While community policing has mixed ratings on one of its intended purposes, that of reducing crime, as a public relations device, intended or not, it has been a howling success."

Youth Outreach Team for the Schools

The next phase of the project/mission was the Youth Outreach Teams for schools. Four officers from patrol (all African-American males) volunteered to work on this phase. The stated goal of this phase was to get close to students and help them understand how the governmental process works and what was going on in Los Angeles during the spring of 1993. Sergeant W.C. indicated that these officers worked on scheduling the United States Attorney's representatives and community policing team into all of the high schools and middle schools in the south end. However, the Youth Outreach Teams faced some resistance. Sergeant W.C. noted:

> The only reservations we ran into were at Denny Middle School where the principal was worried about the officers coming and doing this in uniform. We maintained our position that it needed to be done in uniform to forge communication bonds with the youth in the schools and their police department. The school staff at Rainier Beach High School was resistant and wanted to schedule rebuttal speakers to ensure a fair and impartial presentation of the issues. (p. 17)

Sergeant W.C. also indicated, "All of the major actors met with the entire school staff, and after some candid dialogue, the staff agreed to support the effort of communication with the students" (p. 17).

The process and planning by the South Seattle community police was enormously complicated and labor-intensive, reported Sergeant W.C. For example, they were involved in the neighborhood outreach from March 8 through March 18, 1993, and they were also simultaneously working with the community and the Crime Prevention

Unit planning youth activities for the week of April 5 through April 9. Furthermore, on March 23, 1993, they sent three two-officer teams into Cleveland High School, along with three United States attorneys. It is clear that the western United States Attorney's Office was interested in supporting Youth Outreach Teams in middle and high schools in Seattle.

Critics of community policing and experts of public relations policing contend that this form of outreach provides an opportunity for people to "grass" (tattle) on their neighbors, friends, and enemies (Websdale, 1994). It is important to lay out the specificity of this outreach. Sergeant W.C. wrote:

> This effort continued through April 2, 1993. During that period we sent between three to six two-officer teams into all eleven high schools and middle schools in the South Precinct. We gave a balanced and professional view [sic] of the events in Los Angeles and were very impressed and grateful to the U.S. Attorney's Office and the FBI personnel who assisted in this endeavor. All nine community policing team officers, the four patrol officers, the federal personnel, and school administrators felt it was a very worthwhile program and should be repeated occasionally. During that two-week period, our teams interacted with over 8,000 youth in the south-end schools. (p. 17)

The ability of the South Precinct to work with the SSCPC and its associates explains the power and nature of D.A.R.E.-type programs. These programs are political symbols that are supported by powerful stakeholders both inside and outside of government.

Final Phase of the Project/Mission

It has been suggested that the Seattle Police Department's South Precinct and the South Precinct Community Police Team was subtly involved in the construction of cohesion and regulation of the social system in the central district and the south end. The first parts of this chapter focused on what the community-police team's major actors felt they accomplished by organizing the above project/mission during the important months of March and April of 1993. For example, one officer who participated in this project reported:

The students were initially reserved. However, the students became much more active after we explained that we were not there to make excuses for or take sides in the L.A. issues, just to present the facts. I was surprised to see the number of students who do not n1ve a clear understanding of our judicial system. A large number of students expressed an interest in viewing the inner workings of the Seattle Police Department, i.e., communications and other units. Implementing a program of this nature has unlimited potential in recruitment and community relations efforts. (p. 18)

This point of view helps community policing opponents and proponents understand the benefits of community-oriented policing. Community policing has powerful ideological baggage attached under the rubric of "public education and civics."

This process of reaching out to the community was quite time-consuming, as mentioned earlier. For example, the youth activity portion of the operation was going on daily. Community policing team officers were involved in most of the planning. Other actors provided support and resources. This portion of the project/mission was handled by the Crime Prevention Unit, and the community groups were organized by the South Precinct Community Police Team. The Crime Prevention Unit coordinators worked in decentralized satellite offices around the city and were responsible for working in fixed areas of the city (where the precincts are located).

It was intimated earlier that the Seattle Police Department did not expend monies in its budget to expand community policing. However, monies were found to organize the Community Outreach and Youth Appreciation Week.

The author contends that the purpose of this public relations effort was multi-faceted. First, the most obvious purpose was social control of potentially "disorderly" youth and their supporters. Second, the Rodney King trials triggered outbursts in Los Angeles, and a possible similar reaction by the young people of Seattle was a concern to the police establishment, public officials, and merchants in downtown Seattle.

The question of where the money and resources came from to implement the project/mission is relevant because of what the author learned while researching the politics of community policing in Seattle. According to the internal memo (April 27, 1993):

> [The sergeant] went to the Seattle Police Officer's Guild and obtained $1,000.00 seed money to help fund some of these activities. The Seattle Police Management Association donated $200.00 and [an officer] donated $150.00. Numerous businesses and individuals donated goods and funds to finance the activities. South community policing teams agreed to work the security for the Late Night Recreation programs in the South Precinct if they would expand their hours to have Late Night programs on Wednesday and Thursday, in addition to the normal Friday and Saturday late night programs. (p. 18)

It should be noted that the activities of the project/mission described and outlined above had a social dimension. For example:

> Community policing teams also worked district patrol cars so police officers on the basketball team could get off duty to play in the basketball games between Highpoint Youth and police, and Southwest Community Center and police. South Precinct Officers won the hard fought championship game 97-92 and brought home the trophy. After the game there was pizza, laughter, a midnight swim, and an overnighter. Two community policing team officers volunteered to help chaperon that function. (p. 18)

The activities of the project/mission involved city hall, the chief of police, the Seattle City Council, and, most of all, the local community leaders. Sergeant W.C. wrote:

> During the week preceding Spring Vacation, they [the project committee] obtained 27 signed proclamations from the mayor, ordered picture frames, got 27 signed letters from the Chief of Police explaining Youth Appreciation Week, and hand delivered the plaques and letters to the south-end schools and to the East and North Precincts to deliver to their schools. We also received from the printer in the last few days the large and small activity calendars. We delivered those to all the schools, libraries, and recreations centers. (p. 18)

The South Seattle community came forward with volunteers and donations, and provided some job opportunities and employment leads in West Seattle. The planners of the project/mission organized all of the activities listed above in seven weeks.

The last portion of the project/mission was to strengthen the overall community-police partnership, a goal stated by the writer of the internal memo. Sergeant W.C. provided a personal insight of the mission after it was all over:

> I believe that the cooperation and support this project received from all over the community, police department, mayor's office, and all city departments is a very clear indicator of a very healthy community and police partnership. This project definitely indicated to our community that we have a commitment beyond normal law enforcement, which of course is the very essence of why we now have community police teams. (p. 19)

It is apparent from the latter statement that the leaders of this public education program felt they were doing the right thing by organizing these high-crime neighborhoods and communities. The benefit for the Seattle Police Department was continued legitimacy and consent for their organization.

The conclusion and recommendations offered by the sergeant revealed that the goals were achieved, and suggested what the thrust of the South Seattle police team's future efforts in community policing should be. Specifically, Sergeant W.C. indicated that the goals were met, and that the citizens they interacted with during the youth activity portion of the project/mission were positive. According to Sergeant W.C.'s memo, the South Precinct Community Police Team and associates "had positive interaction with over 15,000 citizens in the South precinct while completing C.P.T. Project 93-1" (p. 19).

Furthermore, Sergeant W.C. credited an officer with providing insight to the mission both internally and externally. The officer was committed to community policing and represented the small cadre of officers who "walk the talk" of community policing in its token form. The following passage helps explain the concerns of the South Seattle middle managers:

> I agree with [the officer] that we made a very substantial step in improving communications with a key element of our society [sic]. The youth are not only a challenge to communicate with now, but they are also the leaders of Seattle tomorrow. The perceptions and impressions we made during this effort will be beneficial for all for years to come. The difficulty in recruiting in certain segments of our

community could be eased if we made serious attempts to reach out
and bring these youth into the police world through tours and more
interaction in the schools. (p. 19)

Sergeant W.C. noted the importance of police public relations
efforts and the potential fruits of such project/missions. Police public
relations have a multiplicity of functions and purposes as indicated by
the sergeant. Most important, such efforts serve to bring about youth
support for the police organization and help in recruiting youth who
were once non-supportive of police projects. Historically, both in
Seattle and in other cities, the police have been involved in Police
Athletic League activities. These activities involved the local YMCA,
the churches, the recreation department, and the police department in
keeping young people involved in non-criminal activities. The sergeant
wrote that there were no real surprises during this project and that the
effort went like clockwork. Moreover, he indicated:

> The citizens were pleased to receive the personal one-on-one attention
> from uniformed police officers in their neighborhoods. Their concerns
> were typical of the concerns of citizens in previous neighborhood
> surveys. The officers all reported extremely positive feelings about
> participating in this outreach. I believe that when we talk about
> bridging the gap with the community that the road runs two ways and
> sometimes our officers feel pretty isolated from the community. (p. 20)

Officers in the South Seattle Precinct felt isolated from the local
community for several reasons. One reason could have been the high
number of officers who live in the suburbs of Seattle. The residents
interviewed felt that since the police officers who patrolled the area did
not live in the community, they had no idea what really takes place at
the grassroots level. In addition, officers had reported feeling hostility
from minorities and unemployed residents of the communities which
they were assigned to police daily (Large, 1993). Research showed that
the police department was over 75 percent non-minority officers, and
they were often called upon to police racially diverse and sometimes
hostile neighborhoods. The residents of the neighborhood perhaps
resented the fact that the policeman had a job while they were
unemployed.

Regarding the long-term impacts of such missions, Sergeant W.C.
said:

One of the far reaching effects of this project is that it seems to have mobilized the city and the community to make a commitment to make Youth Appreciation Week an annual event during Spring Break so the youth will have healthy and fun activities during their vacation. It can only get better year after year, especially if there is adequate time for planning and organization. (p. 20)

One clear description of the project/mission outlined above would be a giant D.A.R.E. program that attempted to include everyone. The mission was multi-faceted. It sought to gain the cooperation and respect of the residents and gangs. It was also an information gathering device. If the police department gained some inside information on gang wannabes or gangs and their activities, the mission would be considered successful.

This project involved serious work and time commitments from the mayor's office, chief of police, community leaders, community groups, Crime Prevention Unit, South Precinct patrol officers, United States Department of Justice, Seattle Parks Department, and South Precinct Community Police Team (Internal memo, April 27, 1993). According to Sergeant W.C.:

The above entities worked harmoniously to successfully complete a seven week project. The implementation and conclusion of this effort is an excellent testament to the value of a committed Community Policing Program. A report of the Crime Prevention's involvement in this project is being prepared by that unit. The majority of the youth activity planning and organization was done by Crime Prevention and the community. Community policing team officers assisted as needed, but the recognition of Crime Prevention in this effort is paramount because it was their expertise as community organizers that made it successful. (p. 21)

The sergeant offered three recommendations after consulting with the participants of the operation:

1. Some organized effort should be made to communicate with the youth in the schools on a large scale more often.
2. Youth Appreciation Week should become an annual project. The lead should be taken by the community and by Crime

Prevention Unit, but the South Precinct Community Police Team should be involved also.

3. Every effort should be made to continue to involve patrol officers in the projects. It provides an invaluable two-way learning process. Not only did the patrol officers bring valuable knowledge and expertise to this project, but many of the students were familiar with them from the officers' daily police duties in and around the schools. They helped to lend realism to the exercise.

Research revealed that the Seattle Police Department felt that efforts should be made to continue similar police education programs. Furthermore, they believed that Youth Appreciation Week should be an integral part of police public relations efforts in low-income and potentially hostile neighborhoods. Sergeant W. C. realized that Youth Appreciation Week should be led primarily by the community, with involvement of the community policing teams, the Crime Prevention Unit of the police department, and patrol officers. He alluded to the feeling that the police had been the experts and leaders during Youth Appreciation Week, whereas it should have been the community leaders and residents in the target area who initiated and led the project.

Summary of the Project

The Community Outreach and Youth Appreciation Week project provided one story of how the Seattle Police Department was involved in public education in the central district and south end community. This researcher's conclusion is that this project was not illustrative of true community policing as espoused by scholars (Goldstein, 1990; Brown, 1993; Trojanowicz, 1993; Robinson et al., 1994). It was exclusive in nature and sought to legitimize the small police specialty teams. Many researchers are critical of the teams because they isolate the officers, and many individuals on the teams become the object of ridicule by patrol officers and middle managers. Many of these teams are used for public relations activities that benefit the police only.

Several conclusions can be drawn regarding the Community Outreach and Youth Appreciation Week and the Seattle Police Department's quest to gain legitimacy in this high-crime area of the city. First, the Seattle Police Department was deeply involved in the development of cohesion and regulation of the social system in the central district and south end neighborhoods, particularly in the school system. As previously stated, many D.A.R.E.-type programs are symbolic and political and are not led by the community. Police specialty units usually lead and direct D.A.R.E.-type programs in public schools. Research showed that the Seattle Police Department actively cultivated and orchestrated positive relationships with the public school system and the young people who might be prone to criminal behavior. Overall, this is a good program, but the point is that the program was not citywide. It took place in only one community, and only involved a handful of officers who were committed to community public relations.

Second, the small community policing teams were holistic in nature. Research revealed that these teams in Seattle were involved in every aspect of social life of public housing dwellers and the low-income communities. This is important because the police become the standard bearers of morality and social control. There were other leaders in the community, for instance, youth club directors, small business owners, ministers, women's advocacy groups, senior citizen groups, etc., who could have stepped forward and been the standard-bearers for the community. It would have been better if the program had been more inclusive of the aforementioned citizens in its planning stages.

Third, community policing was only community police relations in Seattle. The community policing literature suggests that community policing should be more than police public relations. Philosophically, the police should be involved in establishing relationships with community residents and in helping them solve problems nominated by the residents themselves (Goldstein, 1990).

Fourth, the Community Outreach and Youth Appreciation Week, as developed by the Seattle Police Department, was devised as a symbol to show citizens that the organization was doing something about crime in Seattle's low-income and high-crime areas. The mayor's office, the city council, and the police chief did not want the department to be perceived as non-caring by its constituents and by the general public.

LEGITIMIZING SEATTLE'S VERSION
OF COMMUNITY POLICING

The Seattle Police Department's public education program (D.A.R.E.-type program) in the south end neighborhoods was very concerned with legitimizing Seattle's model of community policing. The Community Outreach and Youth Appreciation Week project served essentially to legitimate this model.

Seattle's model of community policing was based not only on truths, but also on several myths. Fleissner et al. (1992:9) claim the following regarding community policing in Seattle: (1) Citizens and police partnerships led to decreases in crime in Seattle, (2) Quarterly crime statistics showed dramatic improvements in the quality of life in the south end, (3) Citizen activity spread throughout the city's other three police precincts, and (4) Community policing was a growing concern throughout the city and a citywide success.

Crime decreased in the city overall, not just in the south end, between 1987 and 1989. These decreases could hardly be attributed to the South Seattle Crime Prevention Council efforts alone. The quarterly crime statistics attributed to that group falsely indicated that the quality of life improved for residents in the south end community. The SSCPC used police statistics to present themselves in a favorable light and to further their political agenda. There was little evidence to suggest that the SSCPC influenced the crime rate or police statistics in precincts citywide. However, the group did influence the development of police teams and a small crime-prevention council in the East Precinct. Many individuals and groups learned the language of community policing from the SSCPC.

Citizen activity aimed at reducing street crime is not new to Seattle. The Crime Prevention Unit in the Seattle Police Department has been around for over 20 years. Also, the department has had community service officers responding to domestic calls since the Law Enforcement Administration Assistance Act of the 1960s. Therefore, community policing was the next step in the progression of crime prevention and policing activities with community-based groups.

Community policing in Seattle was instituted formally in 1990 and was functioning by mid-January of that year with 28 personnel slots filled. Also, a special five-day training academy in the first quarter instructed officers in community policing teams' objectives and problem-solving skills (Fleissner et al., 1992). Out of the five days, one whole day was spent on effective public speaking and public relations. The other four days were spent listening to speakers on such topics as interpersonal skills, street lighting, adult aging services, and city engineering.

The community policing teams were staffed by a sergeant and five officers. One team was assigned to each precinct. Allegedly, these teams worked closely with community groups and organizations to target and try to resolve chronic crime-related situations.

Background of the SSCPC and Its Relationship
with the Seattle Police Department

The SSCPC initially had little rapport with the police department Crime Prevention Unit which was staffed mainly by civilian employees rather than sworn officers. The SSCPC used its resources to push for the reorganization of that unit in 1989. During that period, the Crime Prevention Unit began to assign permanent block watch organizers. Once block watches were established in a neighborhood, the organizers were re-assigned to other neighborhoods. Research showed that the SSCPC utilized its resources and influence with city hall to implement a series of reforms and changes that ultimately led to a politicized version of community policing. Most important, the SSCPC succeeded in bringing together an unlikely coalition of residents and organizations interested in doing something about public crime. This group included the local precinct commanders, splinter crime prevention groups, public housing dwellers, the Seattle Housing Authority, and the Seattle Police Department Crime Prevention Unit.

This coalition of crime fighters led to over three weeks of public education in the schools about the Seattle Police Department and the Rodney King trial in Los Angeles. This police-constructed education effort involved displays of police equipment (including bicycles, horses, and vans), and speeches regarding the Rodney King trial and citizens' responsibilities to their community.

Bureaucratic Add-Ons

An analysis of data (interviews, newspaper analysis, official documents, and crime-prevention telephone logs) found that what was described by community policing proponents in Seattle as a model for community policing was limited in its implementation. What took place organizationally in the Seattle Police Department in 1985-1993 was classic bureaucratic add-ons.

In a National Institute of Justice publication, Goldstein (1993) warns law enforcement scholars that the downside of the newfound popularity of community policing is that it is widely used without any regard for its substance. He states that both political and police leaders are latching onto the label for the positive images it evokes, but do not invest in the concept itself. For example, he states (and the research supports) that some police leaders resist community policing initiatives because of the belief that they constitute an effort to placate an overly demanding and critical segment of the community that is intent on exercising more control over police operations.

What happened in Seattle was true to Goldstein's warnings. This became evident as the Seattle Police Department's resistance to disorganized and vocal central district residents' efforts to implement a version of community policing in their neighborhoods was researched. However, the organized members of the SSCPC had been able to get some of their demands met regarding crime control and prevention in the south end between 1985 and 1993, which led to community policing (Scheingold, 1991).

Goldstein (1993:1) states that "the popularity of the term [community policing] has resulted in its being used to encompass practically all innovations in policing, from the most ambitious to the most mundane, from the most carefully thought-through to the most casual." He goes on to say:

> In the larger public forum, the label is being used in ways that increase public expectations of the police; that create the impression that, somehow, on implementation, community policing will provide a panacea for not only crime, disorder, and racial tension, but many of the other acute problems that plague our urban areas.

As Goldstein's analysis implies, community policing has been increasingly touted by political leaders as the solution to gangs, guns, graffiti, and street violence. No mention is made in the popular rhetoric of community policing of the deep-seated structural problems facing urban municipalities. Robinson et al. (1994) make the point that the word "resource" is not in the community policing dictionary. The urban problems mentioned above are complex and will not be solved by the implementation of community policing programs alone.

Seattle's Variant Form of Community Policing

In Seattle during the period 1985-1993, the mayor's office and the police department fashioned a variant form of community policing that would be acceptable to diverse publics. The extensive purpose of this new program was to do something about crime in several neighborhoods experiencing gun violence and street crimes. The purpose of the community policing teams was to focus on crimes that contributed to physical and social disorder and neighborhood decay (Seattle Police Department Long Range Plan, 1992).

The researcher concludes that the community policing program in Seattle produced no detectable organizational changes in the police department hierarchy, the police department and the mayor's office accepted a 15-Point Plan crafted by an elitist and exclusionary group in the high-crime area, and there was no change in the mission statement of the police department.

In contrast, the researcher found that in Portland, Oregon, the police department changed its mission statement and sought community-wide support in its transition to community policing in the late 1980s. The city had evidenced sharp increases in crime, gangs, and drugs, which strained the resources of the Portland Police Bureau. City officials, in conjunction with the chief, made a decision to develop a five-year plan to operationalize the philosophy of community policing in the entire police bureau (Portland Police Bureau, 1992).

In 1992, community policing in Seattle was defined by department officials as a partnership with residents and neighborhoods to achieve the mission of the police department. To that end, the mission statement was: "To protect and serve the public, enforce the law, protect lives and property, promote and maintain order, and work together on problems of mutual concerns" (Seattle Police Department Long Range Plan, 1992:1). The wording is basically the same and is similar to traditional police departments' mission statements. The "work together on problems of mutual concern" language was new, and has been cited in the police public relations literature since 1990.

In reality, the Seattle Police Department implemented a token form of community policing teams in four precincts citywide. No real commitment to the more transformative goals and philosophy of community policing was evident during the researcher's visits to Seattle during the summer of 1993. The partnership aspect of problem-oriented policing was evident from pamphlets and public relations activities.

Seattle's version of community policing served to legitimate the Seattle Police Department in the eyes of the public and to withstand the potential for outbreaks of violence by youth and their sympathizers. The sergeant of the South Seattle Precinct, working in conjunction with South Seattle Crime Prevention Council leaders, fashioned a noble effort to keep young people busy during spring break. The researcher describes the sergeant's organizing efforts as moral entrepreneurship. He seemed to be interested in doing the "right thing" to prevent crime. He was so committed to the Community Outreach and Youth Appreciation Week that he used his own money in the fund-raising effort. It is hard to be critical of his efforts or those of the small community policing teams. However, when reviewing the entire project/mission, it is clear that the SSCPC used the effort to make itself look good with the local precinct and with officials downtown.

The SSCPC was subtly involved in legitimating the status quo in the south end. Traditionally, the status quo was middle-class homeowners and quiet neighborhoods. This was ideal for real estate interests that constituted the SSCPC membership and supporters. Several of the SSCPC leaders owned the local real estate agency, local newspaper, and private businesses in the low-income/high-crime area enclaves. With the influx of diverse populations, these small business owners and residents felt that their way of life was threatened, and the status quo was being upset by the behavior of street criminals and "riffraff." The SSCPC was involved in helping select targets for police action, working with police officers doing graffiti paint-outs, and serving as the eyes and ears of the police by staffing a hotline for receiving crime information from citizens. The group felt that taking these crime control and crime-prevention actions would preserve the status quo of their neighborhood. It is important to note that the chief of police simultaneously acquiesced to the demands of this resource-rich group and used the group for his own ends.

Under the guise of representing the community, the SSCPC sought to advance its image and influence with the police department, the state legislature, and local south end precinct leaders. This group served an important function in a community with two large public housing projects and a lack of viable grassroots leadership (other than the SSCPC). The SSCPC leaders became experts on community policing for their own political ends.

The relationship that emerged between the Seattle Police Department and the SSCPC could best be described as symbiotic. The department needed legitimacy in the eyes of low-income and minority communities, and the SSCPC leadership had the resources to deliver in the area of crime control public relations and prevention. The Seattle Police Department's D.A.R.E.-type programs were concerned with legitimizing Seattle's model of community policing in the south end community.

THE TALE OF TWO COMMUNITIES (SOUTH END AND CENTRAL DISTRICT)

The Seattle Police Department suffered threats and/or loss of its legitimacy in the eyes of the African-American and low-income communities of Seattle, particularly in the central district, around the Weed & Seed program that was proposed by the mayor in 1992. The police department and governmental agencies wanted to be perceived as fair and as doing something about street crime in both communities. The story below has both race and class implications for community policing programs and their implementation in large cities. The Weed & Seed controversy is the tale of two communities.

Weed & Seed

The Seattle Police Department lost legitimacy in the eyes of the public around the Weed & Seed controversy. The Weed & Seed program was originally opposed by some residents and community-based organizations who objected to the federal proposal and proposed "weeding" tactics of the Seattle Police Department on the grounds of perceived civil liberties and civil rights violations. Residents of the central district had long felt that the Seattle Police Department and local government officials did not take their concerns about street crime seriously. Many government officials did not feel that the central district was influential enough to make a difference politically. Therefore, the central district received the spoils of the downtown political system. Consequently, residents of the central district and the south end had different perceptions of the Seattle Police Department and of local government officials.

The organized and more middle-class-appearing businessmen and women of the SSCPC commanded the attention and respect of the police. The central district residents were perceived as an underclass by the police department, media, and local government officials. The idea of "weeding them out" seemed to be the politically appropriate thing to do. The central district (target neighborhood) is an area of 220 city blocks covering 1.2 square miles. The population at the time of this research was about 12,000 residents, including a high concentration of African-Americans (47 percent) and Asians (15 percent). This area was blighted and economically depressed and was considered one of the city's high-crime districts (Seattle Police Department Long Range Plan, 1992:18).

In Dick Lilly's 1992 article in the *Seattle Times*, "Attack Crime or Harass Teens? Central District Groups Protest 'Weed and Seed' Grant," he wrote, "Some African-Americans in the Central District are insulted and angry over a possible federal crime-fighting grant to Seattle— Operation Weed and Seed—which they say would be a tool for police to harass Black teens" (March 24, 1992:B3). Later (March 27, 1992:A1), in "City Urged to Bury Weed and Seed Plan. They're gunning for Black youths says teenager," Lilly quotes one youth who expresses a view of law enforcement shared by many in the African-American community. However, Kathi Lehr of Seattle wrote to the editor of the *Seattle Times* (April 6, 1992:A11), arguing:

> The Weed and Seed grant for the Central Area is a chance to support grassroots efforts in that community. As a public high school teacher of young people, I strongly support this potential resource [Weed and Seed]. It can only help us reduce crime and upgrade our neighborhood.

The debate continued. Stuart Wong wrote to the *Seattle Times* (April 6, 1992:A11) stating, "The city of Seattle should seize the opportunity for the Weed and Seed aid." Wong was critical of citizens appearing at the Seattle City Council hearing, and he stated they "missed the point of the federal aid." He wrote, "If we don't get the aid, another city will get it. Violent crime is on the rise, partly due to drug trafficking. Many of our children are dying by conscious choice or misfortune due to drugs. Even one death is too many." Robert Brown also wrote the *Seattle Times* (April 6, 1992:A11), arguing:

> Weed and Seed should be looked at as a program that's meant to deal with crime, and that it is not race-oriented or racist. . . .Safe neighborhoods are safe not because they are rich or white, but because the community is truly part of the law-enforcement team.

The *Seattle Times* finally offered an editorial on the Weed & Seed controversy titled: "Weeding and Seeding: Local Control Key to Success, Support" (April 7, 1992:A14):

> A $1.1 million federal law-enforcement grant to Seattle for use in fighting urban crime is cause for celebration, not alarm. . . .For weeks critics have claimed that if Seattle is approved for the horribly named Weed and Seed program, it would likely result in the harassment of Central Area African-American residents as it would be to reduce crime.

The Weed & Seed label attached to the project by the federal government caused problems for the mayor as he proceeded to sell it to central district residents. The *Seattle Times* supported the Weed & Seed program, and editors stated, "Critics should welcome the new dollars and work with their communities and neighbors to make sure that they are used wisely as city officials have promised" (April 7, 1992:A14). The editorial further read:

> Although slow to get aboard the concept of having police work more closely with communities, which is the essence of community policing, there are some recent success stories around the city. Residents and business people in both the Rainier Valley and Denny Regrade have praised police for their cooperation.

On April 6, 1992, Mayor Rice officially announced the awarding of the grant and indicated that it was for the inner city of Seattle. In response to critics, the mayor stated (Lilly, *Seattle Times*, April 6, 1992:B1):

> We really view this grant as an extension of our existing community policing efforts, providing more resources for the community and our police to utilize in their joint efforts to promote neighborhood safety.

The mayor indicated that a Community Advisory Council of residents and business owners from the central district would provide input and oversight for law enforcement and social service initiatives under the grant for the city of Seattle.

The Central District

Central district residents have traditionally had problems with federal grants and the management of poverty programs at the local level; for instance, many citizens in the central district had negative experiences with poverty programs of the 1960s. Other citizens were unsure of the sincerity of the federal government and questioned the motives of the local elected leadership. The Weed & Seed project linked law enforcement and poverty programs with federal government involvement in local crime control efforts. Specifically, the weeding operations were coordinated by the commander of the East Precinct from a special command center. Weeding involved activities of the Community Police Team (CPT), Anti-Crime Team (ACT), the gang unit, and narcotics unit in coordination with the FBI and other federal and state agencies (Seattle Police Department Long Range Plan, 1992). The mayor indicated that the purpose of the grant was to fight crime and augment social programs in the central district. He emphasized that the Seattle Weed & Seed program would be controlled locally. A local citizens' advisory group would monitor the program. However, some citizens remained skeptical that the Weed & Seed program could be adapted for Seattle. It is the conclusion of this researcher that the Weed & Seed program was really no different from earlier federal grants and programs; it just had a new, fancy title.

Weed & Seed had controversial strings tied to it. Both local monies and federal monies were matched for long-term planning and growth. The central district is the part of town that has the greatest land value and potential for developers.

Seattle Times reporter Dick Lilly captured some community skepticism when he wrote the article: "Weed and Seed Skeptics Remain Despite Federal Grant—Mayor Still Has to Sell Program to Central Area" (April 7, 1992:B1). Although the mayor announced that two-thirds of the money would go to crime-fighting programs, and the rest would attack the causes of crime and be spent on programs such as education and job training, Lilly wrote that the Justice Department's description of the program, along with its insensitive sounding name, conjured up images of federal law enforcement agents rounding up individuals from street corners.

One community organizer, Arnette Holloway, was successful in obtaining signatures from over forty groups to contest the implementation of Weed & Seed in Seattle. Holloway succeeded in politicizing the federal Weed & Seed program in Seattle by arguing that the FBI would be patrolling the streets of Seattle. Furthermore, she was able to incite dormant and disorganized community groups into taking on city hall around the Weed & Seed program (personal interview, July 5, 1993).

The mayor was forced to change his position about the horribly named garden program several times. Community residents were suggesting that maybe the central district needed to be seeded first and weeded later. The implementation of community policing was blocked for over nine months as the city council convened hearings and the mayor went back to Washington, D.C. to gain clarification from the Bush administration about the true nature of Weed & Seed. Holloway and her supporters questioned why Weed & Seed could not be implemented citywide. She questioned placing the federal program in the central district, which had a history of bad police-community relations.

One central district leader indicated to Lilly that after a heated city council hearing and a flood of calls pro and con to city hall, Mayor Rice needed to use his personal prestige to calm central district community fears. That leader went on to suggest that the uproar over Weed & Seed set back police-community relations in the central district several years (Lilly, April 7, 1992).

The loss of legitimacy for the mayor and police department over Weed & Seed may be viewed as evenly distributed. Could residents of Seattle believe the United States Attorney, the mayor, or the police chief when they stated publicly that the weeding portion of the grant would concentrate on the community policing concept and getting the most violent and dangerous offenders off the street? Although the Seattle community was equally divided over the Weed & Seed controversy, publicly the central district residents and its vocal leaders were vehemently against it.

Don Williamson, a columnist for the *Seattle Times*, wrote (April 19, 1992:A19):

> Police Chief Pat Fitzsimons (Seattle Police Department) says that there will be no sweeps of street corners and no harassment and abuse of power by law enforcement officials. Also, Mayor Rice, to whom the police chief is answerable for his job, says that he wants to make the Seattle streets safe for people to walk and that community input will be the driving force behind Weed and Seed.

Many residents of the targeted neighborhoods felt that the federal government's Weed & Seed program would initiate tough law enforcement activities which would infringe upon the civil rights of the local citizens. Williamson wrote that the ACLU of Washington State pointed to the potential of having one set of laws (federal) for the central district, and another set (local and state) for the rest of the city. The latter comments by Williamson were the main contentions of anti-Weed & Seed activists. Pro-Weed & Seed activists supported the Seattle Police Department. The ACLU took the side of the anti-Weed & Seed activists and politicized the issue of police behavior in the central district. Mothers Against Police Harassment forcefully predicted that unrestrained law enforcement activity related to the Weed & Seed program would trample constitutional protections (Williamson, April 19, 1992:A19). Williamson ended the column by stating that Seattle citizens must start trusting each other. He suggested that citizens would have to trust the mayor, the police chief, the ACLU, and Mothers Against Police Harassment, and keep agitating and pointing out alleged police official violations.

Damita Brown and Amy Kratz of Seattle wrote an engaging letter to the *Seattle Times* (April 26, 1992:A19) indicating that the Weed & Seed money should be used to provide part-time jobs for youth. Both of these individuals voiced displeasure at the mayor and police chief for supporting the federal Weed & Seed program. Specifically, they wrote that the city of Seattle has failed to provide jobs, education, and recreational facilities for young inner city children. They argued that Weed & Seed was blatantly racist and would do nothing to eliminate unemployment or the high dropout rate among African-Americans and disadvantaged youth. Ms. Brown and Ms. Kratz concluded the letter by writing:

> The implementation of racist police policies will not reduce desperation in the local community, and such programs exacerbate violence and discourage cooperative efforts between city officials and an economically destitute community.

On May 1, 1992, in response to the verdict in the Rodney King case (Birkland, May 1, 1992:A1), dozens of merchants in downtown Seattle boarded up broken storefront windows and counted their merchandise losses after looting and vandalism. In Seattle, about 45 African-American, white, and Hispanic individuals were booked on a variety of charges (after the Rodney King verdict), including assault, arson, property damage, burglary, failure to disperse, and interfering with firefighters (Birkland, May 1, 1992:A1). In all, 180 people were arrested, of which 149 were adults, reported the *Seattle Times* (Birkland, May 1, 1992:A1). At a press conference called by the mayor, the police chief indicated that about 85 police officers "used remarkable restraint" in confrontations with "opportunists" (Birkland, May 1, 1992:A1). The chief's comments referred to disorderly rioters breaking into stores just for the fun of it. Furthermore, it was believed that these people really had no beef with city hall or with the local police. They just wanted to take advantage of merchants and carry out criminal activity. City council member Margaret Pageler, head of the Public Safety Committee, stated after the mini-rebellion that the city pledged to work with the business community to restore order and maintain the downtown area as "vibrant and welcoming" to visitors (Birkland, May 1, 1992:A1). Many Weed & Seed advocates saw the rioting as an opportunity to promote the adoption of the Weed & Seed program in the central district.

Weed & Seed's most vocal advocate was Mrs. Chris Evers-Aguilar. As leader of the Garfield Community Council, she offered unqualified support for the mayor and the police department. Specifically, her group wrote the *Seattle Times* (November 13, 1992:A9):

> We recognize that Weed and Seed as conceived by the Bush administration is not a solution to all the problems confronting the Central Area. But a "Seattle solution" can incorporate Weed and Seed as a start in the important process of developing the Central Area into the type of neighborhood committed residents desire.

Mrs. Evers-Aguilar asserted that relations in the central district between police and African-Americans were very poor. However, she supported Weed & Seed because the program added emphasis to community policing in Seattle. She described community policing as a program that was already at work improving relationships in the central district, and pointed to the success of several community policing team officers in the East Precinct.

Research that was conducted showed that the Seattle Police Department suffered threats and a loss of its legitimacy in the eyes of the African-American and low-income communities in the central district, particularly around the federal Weed & Seed program. The central business district where these citizens were concentrated was not particularly important to the mayor's re-election efforts because, historically, he only garnered around 30 percent of the residents' votes. The police chief, likewise, had a history of poor relationships with central district community-based organizations, hence, he had nothing to lose by promoting Weed & Seed. He could always point to his friends and supporters in the south end, specifically the SSCPC and their loyal supporters, in the face of claims of insensitivity. The SSCPC helped his push for community policing, a push that led to the Seattle Police Department being labeled as a model for community policing.

Doing Something About Crime

With the advent of Weed & Seed, the police chief and the mayor agreed to expand the East Precinct community policing team to work extensively with the target neighborhoods in the central district. Also, they agreed to develop new multi-lingual crime-prevention brochures to address the diverse neighborhoods. The chief and local government officials wanted to be perceived as sensitive and supportive, and wanted to show that they were doing something about street crime.

The chief was impressed with the partnership thrust of community policing because it illustrated the police department strategically managing police resources. He felt that the partnership went two ways. In general, he felt the communities should be raising law-abiding children, and educational institutions should be promoting civic virtues and law-abiding behavior. The chief blamed the wider system of social institutions, including the family and the schools, for the street crime problem. He attributed the crime problem in Seattle to a failed criminal justice system that was not being hard enough on criminals, not on an irresponsible or unaccountable police department.

These two neighborhoods, the central district and the south end, had different perspectives on the need for crime reduction and community-oriented policing in Seattle. Overall, the SSCPC and south end leaders were organized and had powerful support. The central district, largely made up of service-oriented businesses, was disorganized and experienced high numbers of arrests for Part 1 offenses, and was constantly patrolled by the Seattle Police Department. Weed & Seed was implemented in this neighborhood despite community-based opposition.

The mayor's office and the police department publicly indicated that the Seattle "weed" expenditures would be under control of the mayor and city council. Furthermore, no weeding dollars would pay for federal or state law enforcement, and there would be no FBI or other federal control of Seattle law enforcement strategies. The mayor publicly worked hard to explain to community leaders and residents in the central district that the federal government would only get involved in city matters as they related to emergency situations. Finally, the mayor wanted community residents to know there would be no street sweeps or disparate law enforcement in the central district. The mayor was constantly under pressure to prove that even though he is African-American and did not live in the central district, he supported their aspirations.

According to the mayor, the Community Police Team mission was to work with the community to reduce violence and drug crimes in the neighborhood. Organized community resistance to Seattle's implementation of Weed & Seed led to one important change. Instead of the 80 percent weed and 20 percent seed money originally asked for in the SPD planning department's grant proposal, the mayor's new proposal to the federal government was 47 percent weed and 53 percent seed. Vocal community organizers were able to get city hall to drop the requirement of direct Justice Department involvement in Seattle law enforcement. Specifically, the original federal Weed & Seed prospectus suggested frightening and repressive law enforcement measures such as street sweeps. Community leaders, as disorganized as they may have been, gained support from the nine-member city council which finally voted six to three to approve Seattle's version of Weed & Seed. Only with a new president and a new United States attorney general in 1993 did community residents organizing against Weed & Seed change their perspective of federal criminal justice programs.

Obviously, the Seattle Police Department was subtly involved in the politics of community policing, and Seattle's version of community policing had both social control mechanisms and public relations components. The ostensible purpose of these public relations schemes and race relations programs was to placate local community leaders, neighborhood organizations, business leaders, and police officers into police-driven strategies that have limited community support and involvement.

The politics of community policing are ideological, insofar as they focus on the police department maintaining fragile consent and legitimacy from the government. The politics of community policing helps enumerate why the mayor and city officials put Weed & Seed in the central district of Seattle and linked it to neighborhood betterment. The department was involved in organizational add-ons, which means that when the Seattle Police Department had a chance to obtain federal money, it attempted to appropriate the funds to add to its budget. The major characteristics of crime-prevention activities and crime control aspects of the Seattle Police Department signal organizational add-ons. For example, the department sought and won money for neighborhood watch, block watch, residential and business watch, the Mountain Bike Patrol, civil abatement process, and drug-free zones. The Seattle Police Department's efforts in the south end helped to implement the Community Outreach and Youth Appreciation Week to help improve their legitimacy. It gained funding for the Weed & Seed program in the central district. The commitment to community policing was a panacea at the political level in Seattle. The local political elites' expressions of dissatisfaction with the rise in the recorded crime rate led the department to do whatever necessary to deal with the crime problem symbolically.

Community policing as a proactive policy has numerous dimensions, and they are used sequentially; for example, cooptation, cooperation, consultation (when appropriate), collaboration (with supportive groups), and consensus (when appropriate). The end result is subtly to create consent and maintain legitimacy from all classes in the community for the police organization and their loyal supporters.

CHAPTER 4

Urban Political Processes

This chapter examines how urban political processes affected the development of community policing in Seattle. This level of analysis involves the processes by which urban politicos, or actors, shape their responses to social problems and, in this particular case, the politics of crime control. The existing literature on urban political process provides a framework for understanding how the Seattle government responded to the problems posed by crime, including problems of legitimacy.

The works of urban economists such as Peterson (1981), Katznelson (1981), Walzer (1986), Elkin (1987), Erie (1988), Judd (1988), Stone (1989), and Barnes (1990) are particularly useful for the study of community policing in Seattle. This level of analysis focuses on political-economic processes and reveals the relationship between economic and political power in a society where controls and the use of property are largely private matters. Private ownership is not entirely private, because many private businesses have powerful public linkages. Indeed, in a capitalist economic system, the political processes often revolve around issues of what is private and what is not private, and the distinction between the two spheres is subject to constant negotiation (Walzer, 1986).

Local governments have vastly increased their power and responsibilities in the public safety and law enforcement arenas. In an eight-year span, the Seattle Police Department budget increased by $51,358,631.00 (Fleissner et al., 1992). Public safety accounted for over 50 percent of the 1990-1993 adopted budgets. Even though the budget increased, very little of the money was invested in the community policing programs implemented in the south end and central district (Reed, 1995).

Urban governments are vested with the authority to act collectively in the name of citizens (Judd and Kantor, 1992). The power and authority of government is a political resource that private actors and institutions do not possess. Urban government has the authority to make and apply decisions that are binding upon all segments of society (Weber, 1947; Nordlinger, 1981). Ideally, in a democratic system, governmental decisions are legitimated primarily through processes that are intended to allow for participation by citizens and their representatives (Judd and Kantor, 1992).

Several policing scholars offer a critical perspective on the political economy side of community policing. Cain (1973), Hall et al. (1978), and Gilroy (1982) all discuss the politics of policing. While Brogden (1982) examines the cooperative nature of community policing, Cain and Sadigh (1982) look at systems of social control, and Brogden, Jefferson, and Walklate (1988), the policing of social crises and of powerless minorities. These authors illustrate the ongoing discussion of political and economical influences on the community policing movement.

According to Judd and Kantor (1992), not all political interests can make a claim on public authorities. Businesses and corporations have a privileged position in every capitalist society. They make demands on and ask for special consideration from political leaders with regularity. Many writers (Lindblom, 1977; Elkin, 1987; Domhoff, 1986) support the notion that in all capitalist nations, society depends upon the ability of the private sector to provide employment and income for citizens and revenue for urban and state government. Political scientists have attempted to explain the pressures on local government to produce jobs, present their city as an attractive place to live, and maintain public safety.

Urban political processes are influenced by both urban political economists and contemporary scholars of the police. Explaining change in the last decade in urban America, urbanist John J. Harrigan (1993) contends the federal government has continued its retreat from the economics and fiscal problems of central cities. He states that most visibly blacks, women, and Hispanics have entered the forefront of urban politics and have been elected mayors of major United States cities such as New York, Chicago, Philadelphia, San Antonio, San Francisco, and Houston. In 1994, the mayor of Seattle was African-

American, and the city council was predominantly female. Harrigan (1993) finds that these major cities have not served as the melting pot of old for minorities.

Seattle, however, is unlike those other cities described above, as it has an economy that is robust, vibrant, and future-oriented. However, from 1985 to 1993, the city government was experiencing a slight decline in resources (taxes) due to fluctuations in the local and national economies. Serious felony crime was increasing, particularly violent crime such as murder. The Seattle Police Department, the mayor's office, and the city council, under public pressure, sought to implement crime control policies that city and police department leaders found politically acceptable while maintaining fragile consent, legitimacy, and re-election opportunities.

Two propositions may be advanced here. First, the Seattle Police Department faced both *internal* and *external* political pressures to implement community policing, and, second, *buffers* such as consultative committees served to co-opt the community into acceptance of community policing (Gordon, 1987).

Several questions arise from this discussion: Did the Seattle government (the mayor's office, city council, and Seattle Police Department) face any form of political, management, or fiscal crisis or pressures shortly before or after the community policing teams were created in January 1990? And if so, in what ways did this crisis or pressure shape the development and implementation of community policing in Seattle? Also, is there any evidence to show that members of the Seattle government (police, city council, or mayor's office) established buffers to enhance their image in the eyes of the general public or with special interest groups? (For this discussion, "buffers" refer to the programs and activities used by Seattle government officials and the Seattle Police Department to subtly cushion the blow of the social and political contradictions inherent in a capitalist society.) Some minor questions also rise from this discussion: Did Seattle officials (the mayor, city council, and police chief) have the confidence, trust, and/or support of their constituency? And, what was the public response to urban politicos' (actors') failure to do something about crime?

There appears to have been both *internal* and *external* political pressures on Seattle city government, specifically, the mayor's office, city council, and Seattle Police Department, to do something about street crime. Internal and external political pressures forced the Seattle Police Department to create what has come to be defined as a model for community policing. It appears that one of the reasons community policing was implemented was to placate a rising urban underclass, and the department only implemented public relations policing and a token form of community policing. These conclusions are based on the following: (1) the Buracher and Associates study of the Seattle Police Department (Fleissner et al., 1991), (2) internal and external audits, (3) South Seattle Crime Prevention Council hotline reports (personal communications, 1990), and (4) central district leaders pressuring the police department to take their crime and police agenda seriously.

It seems likely that buffers were set up by Seattle city government (the mayor's office, the city council, and the police department) to offset pressures on the police department to do something about crime. The SSCPC may have been used as a buffer, and former Judge Terrence Carroll's appointment as internal auditor to deal with allegations of police malpractice may have been another.

To examine Seattle's model for community policing in depth, it is necessary to discuss Seattle's city politics, as reflected in the mayor's speeches, the composition of the city council, Seattle Police Department memorandum, public documents, and interviews conducted during the summer of 1993. The Seattle local community and human agency is probed via public documents, books, articles, and interviews conducted during the summer of 1993 to explore the local community's reaction to street crime. Urban political processes theory and data tell the story of community policing's emergence and implementation. Community policing image was contemplated as the solution to the crime problem in Seattle during the period 1985-1993. It is theorized that Seattle city government symbolically responded to the crime problem by implementing a token form of community policing. Theories and data show that community policing was a political response to deep-seated structural problems facing the city. These structural problems were manifest in the south end, the central district, and in pockets of downtown Seattle.

Seattle city politics, the local community and human agency, and community policing are discussed as a panacea to the crime problem in Seattle. Specifically, this study will focus on (1) centers of power and authority in Seattle, (2) the police chief and his administrative duty to control potentially volatile situations, (3) community policing influence regarding low-income communities, (4) federal government money for crime and gang prevention, (5) segments of the public and their opposition to government and reactive policing, (6) city government officials' use of community policing to improve image and legitimation, and (7) the way citizens organized to put pressure on city council members, the mayor, and the police chief to do something about crime.

SEATTLE CITY GOVERNMENT

In a review of the best cities for business, Bill Saporito of *Fortune* magazine (November 2, 1992:40) indicated that these cities are the ones with the workers, services, and other support systems that most enhance the ability of companies to compete globally. Seattle was named by that author as the top city in the United States to do business. Saporito stated that Seattle's manufacturing competitiveness, workforce sophistication, technological content, and natural resource base show that it is headed toward what one civic leader described as "an international franchise."

Such mythology about Seattle is legendary. For instance, Seattle is viewed by residents as a city at ease with diversity and as the place that practices process-oriented politics. In respect to diversity, some locals have defined Seattle's form of diversity and politics as the illusion of inclusion where African-Americans, Asian-Americans, and Hispanics are included in the decision-making loop. Part of the mythology perpetuated by chamber of commerce brochures and the media is that pigmentation does not matter, and the content of one's character is more important. The politics are defined as the type where local leaders seek all parties' views when making community decisions. The downside of this process-oriented politics is that it takes time for all of the actors to make important decisions.

In validation of this perpetual mythology, four of the mayor's State of the City addresses to the city council and the people of Seattle are presented and analyzed. These speeches add to the mythology of Seattle and the illusion of inclusion. They are important because they illustrate process-oriented politics, decision-making, public safety, and the dynamics of the urban political processes in Seattle.

The State of the City 1990-1993

Mayor Norm Rice's first State of the City speech occurred on July 22, 1990, before the city council and other city officials. He took the time to step back and look at the bigger picture, and discussed his official meetings with Nelson Mandela and the lighting of the torch to begin the

Goodwill Games in Seattle. The mayor described the city of Seattle as one big family and indicated, "Like every family, Seattle is made up of lots of different individuals—singles, couples, single parents, street families, and gay families. From the newborn infant to the elders who helped shape this city. An entire rainbow of ethnic and cultural backgrounds" (Rice, 1990).

What problem did the family of Seattle face, according to the mayor? He indicated that just like every big family, "we've all got to pull together to help the less fortunate members of our family. For the sad fact is, the state of the city in Seattle depends a great deal on who you are" (Rice, 1990). The mayor recognized the social political reality of the city of which he became the first African-American mayor. For instance, first he outlined housing as one of the major problems facing the city. Second, he indicated that education was an important issue. Third, he discussed issues of life and death and indicated that back in 1986, the infant mortality rate among blacks in Seattle was more than double that of the white infant mortality rate. He noted that the infant mortality rate in Seattle was even higher than that rate among blacks in New York City.

The mayor finally spoke about law enforcement and public safety in Seattle. He indicated that when one talks about making Seattle a place where every citizen can thrive, one has to talk about public safety. Specifically, he indicated that public safety goes hand in hand with education, housing, and human services. He reported that it was his job to give the police the tools they need to do their jobs. "Tools to deal with gangs . . . drugs . . . and crime that affects every part of this city, and on the other hand, it is my job to hold the police accountable if they are abusing their role" (Rice, 1990). He stated emphatically, "If there is a problem between our police department and our community, I'm not going to run away from that problem, I'm going to fix it. The buck stops here" (Rice, 1990).

On June 24, 1991, the mayor presented his second State of the City address. He was as optimistic as ever and indicated, "As I travel around the city, I have a feeling that everything is coming together. It's an exciting time. It's a new decade full of hope and promise. . . . There's a spirit of confidence and optimism throughout the city. . . . My message today for every Seattle resident is 'the best is yet to come'" (Rice, 1991). The mayor recognized that there was a downside to the state of the city, and indicated that some people may look at the last few months and say that "anxiety and cynicism have replaced hope and optimism. Some people may look at the city's budget problems and say 'the worst is yet to come.' I don't buy that doom and gloom thinking" (Rice, 1991). The mayor remained upbeat and indicated, "When I look around this city, I see all kinds of ideas and creativity and commitment in our neighborhoods" (Rice, 1991).

The focus of this speech was on the spirit of growth and how it was alive in Seattle. He indicated that the 1990 census showed that Seattle's overall population had jumped from 490,000 in 1980 to an estimated 535,000 in 1990, an increase of nearly 10 percent over the past decade alone. The mayor reiterated his diversity theme, and indicated, "Together, we . . . sent a powerful message that Seattle is a city that cares about diversity and that bigotry has no place in our community" (Rice, 1991).

He also reported that in the area of public safety, the crime rate was down for the third year in a row and major crimes were down by 11 percent since 1987. The mayor mentioned drug-free zone initiative, reporting that the police had arrested sixty people for violating drug-free zone laws.

> Twenty of those cases have already gone through the courts, and the city is batting a thousand. Twenty cases—twenty convictions, with an average sentence of $4^1/2$ years. That's almost double the normal sentence, because they were dealing around our schools. (Rice, 1991)

The mayor gave credit to young people for taking the lead against drug dealing. For example, he noted that young people helped to organize block watches and drug-free rallies. He spoke briefly about the Seattle Police Department, and argued:

> Even if we had the money to put a police officer on every corner, we still wouldn't solve all of our public safety issues. Issues like crime and poverty and education are all inter-related. One-dimensional solutions simply won't work any more. However, we need a strong police presence and we're going to maintain that presence. (Rice, 1991)

The mayor went on to say that 10,000 men and women work for the city of Seattle and that budget shortfalls exist, and that there is a need to streamline city government in the months ahead.

The mayor's third State of the City speech was on January 27, 1992. He took the time to recognize the city council president, George Benson, and said that he was "the conductor on the trolley of our collective future" (Rice, 1992). He discussed the rich diversity of the city council and Seattle neighborhoods and how the diversity set Seattle apart. He indicated that the United States was facing some deep divisions and that the city of Seattle was facing a number of bewildering changes, such as explosive population growth, ever-increasing diversity among citizens, greater awareness of the environment, and a greater recognition of the rights of groups that were formerly ignored. He spoke of the uncertain future of both the Seattle Mariners American League Baseball Team, and of Frederick and Nelson (department store). In this speech he discussed public safety and economic security. With regard to public safety, he indicated that it was virtually impossible to have great schools or strong community-based economic development without a strong, comprehensive commitment to public safety. Most important, he suggested, "We need to further enhance our community policing strategies, to restore a sense of public confidence and involvement and to complement the efforts of our officers" (Rice, 1992). Finally, he stated, "We need to strengthen the links between public safety agencies at every level . . . federal, state, county, and city . . . to improve our ability to deter, apprehend, and prosecute anyone who engages in criminal activity" (Rice, 1992).

On February 1, 1993, the mayor gave his fourth State of the City speech. Speaking of the economy of Seattle, the mayor indicated:

> We've kept our city on a positive course, despite a severe national recession and a devastating slowdown in our revenues. We've taken a hard look at our priorities, and we've refocused our scarce resources to address the most pressing challenges facing our community. (Rice, 1993)

He reiterated one theme that weaves throughout all of the above-mentioned speeches, stating, "We've enhanced Seattle's reputation for innovation and quality of life, in the face of ever-increasing challenges and ever-tightening resources" (Rice, 1993). The mayor wanted the citizens to know that he did not want Seattle to be a city of haves and have-nots. He strongly stated that he wanted "a city where every child has a chance to learn, where every man and woman has the skills to find a good job, and where every individual has a home and the basic necessities of life" (Rice, 1993).

The mayor mentioned some problems in the political economy. For instance, he noted, "Last week's announcement of major cutbacks at Boeing has struck fear into thousands of families, and sent shock waves through our entire regional economy" (Rice, 1993).

The speech had three themes. First, he discussed creating a better employment climate within the city of Seattle. Second, he discussed employment services. Finally, he outlined a familiar theme, which he called "community capacity building" (Rice, 1993).

In the areas of public safety and law enforcement, this speech differed from previous ones. No mention was made of the Seattle Police Department, the Weed & Seed controversy of 1992, or the drug-free zones. He spoke largely in generalities about:

> the nationwide recession, the fall-out from twelve years of Federal neglect, tension and unrest due to the Gulf War and the L.A. verdict, the worse [sic] flooding in our region's history, followed by the worst drought in our region's history—the Fates have packed an entire century of challenges into three short years. (Rice, 1993)

The mayor was optimistic in this speech, because he indicated, "We have a potential partner in the White House" (Rice, 1993). He closed the speech by mentioning that the state had a new governor and a state legislature that seemed eager to tackle the tough issues. He declared the following: "As our new president challenged the nation, let me challenge everyone in this region. This is our time. Let us embrace it" (Rice, 1993).

The mayor's background in the political arena and financial sector helped him organize a coherent response to his various constituents in the city. He was formerly on the city council before being elected mayor.

Composition and Powers of the City Council

The city council is Seattle's elected legislature. The nine members determine city policy through the enactment of ordinances and the adoption of resolutions. Council members are elected at large to four-year terms through citywide elections held in odd-numbered years. The council is non-partisan, and derives its powers from the 1946 City

Charter and the laws and Constitution of the state of Washington. The council authorizes public improvements and expenditures, provides for public safety and health, adopts regulations, levies taxes, controls the finances and property of the city, and performs many related legislative tasks. All ordinances enacted by the council are subject to a mayoral veto, which may be overridden by a vote of six council members (personal communication, 1993). In 1993, there were six women and three men on the city council. The council was composed of Caucasians, African-Americans, and Asian-Americans.

This information is vital because it illustrates the diversity of Seattle city politics as council members interact with the mayor and police chief around public policy issues. Both the deputy mayor and chair of the Public Safety Committee were interviewed by this researcher regarding community policing and the Weed & Seed program. It was learned from one source that the police chief was not fond of elected officials and distrusted their motives, especially regarding policing and law enforcement.

SEATTLE POLICE DEPARTMENT

The Seattle Police Department is an integral part of the urban political processes of the city, deeply involved in a merger of traditional policing and a token form of community policing. Trojanowicz (1991) indicated that the most obvious difference between community policing and traditional policing is that community policing involves average citizens directly in the police process, whereas traditional policing patronizes the community by setting up the police as the experts who have all the answers to community problems.

Public relations material obtained regarding the Seattle Police Department in 1993 showed that it was wholeheartedly embracing the new philosophy of community policing. The annual reports and brochures suggest that the concept in Seattle emphasizes innovative methods to impact crime and the resultant fear within the community. Furthermore, citizens and police in Seattle were presented as forming a partnership to identify factors which support crime and implement solutions that solve the problems rather than just the symptoms. These documents note that community policing teams were implemented as a new program within the Seattle Police Department in 1990. An internal memorandum obtained from the planning department in 1993 evaluated their performance during the first year (personal communication, 1993).

The memorandum claimed that the department's community policing teams were a key and initial component of the Seattle Police Department-wide community policing program. The reports suggested that the community policing teams were successfully implemented in Seattle in full accord with the formal declaration of the program philosophy. The stated objective and mission of the community policing teams in Seattle was (Seattle Police Department 1991-1995 Long Range Plan, 1992):

> Restore the desired quality of life within the community, by resolving neighborhood problems with traditional and non-traditional police tactics, in close interaction with citizens and other governmental agencies.

Community policing in Seattle allegedly augments the traditional police mission of crime control with an effective partnership with the community. The public relations material claimed that citizens help in Seattle's version of community policing by identifying their concerns about crime, social disorder, and neighborhood decay" (Seattle Police Department 1991-1995 Long Range Plan, 1992). For example, SSCPC hotline reports illustrated that many citizens in the south end were involved in calling the police department about "illegal drug sales, gang activity, prostitution, noise disturbance, trespassing, loitering, graffiti, and abandoned vehicles." The SSCPC gathered the hotline reports from July 1990 to November 1990. The hotline was established and data was compiled by the SSCPC to support its claim for some form of community-oriented policing in the south end.

The purpose of the community policing teams in the south end was to pioneer the department into a full-fledged form of community policing. All of the community policing teams were organized and functioning by mid-January 1990, with all 28 personnel slots filled. A special 48-hour training academy instructed them in community policing team objectives and problem-solving skills. The first-year report included glowing accomplishments of the community policing teams. For example, in 1990, Seattle's four community policing teams attended 680 community meetings, made 1,229 school visits and over 9,000 neighborhood and business contacts, and conducted 1,760 projects and cases in coordination with citizens (Seattle Police Department 1991-1995 Long Range Plan, 1992).

Robinson, Scaglion, and Olivero (1994) and Trojanowicz (1989) remind readers that community policing provides a means of gathering superior intelligence that allows police to identify areas at risk, including the level of threat in those areas and the weaknesses and strengths within the local community. Seattle's version of community policing involved gathering information from the community about the level of crime in the community by utilizing police surveys.

One survey conducted by the Seattle Police Department gathered information about police services and needs from citizens throughout the city (Seattle Police Department Long Range Plan, 1992). Approximately 8,700 community surveys were distributed and about 26 percent were returned. The SPD reported that the purpose of the survey was to provide the citizens with an opportunity to voice their concerns about crime in their neighborhoods and to indicate their satisfaction with the job that the Seattle Police Department was doing. There were two different formats to the survey: an eight-page questionnaire was sent to community and business groups, agencies serving women and minority groups, and block watch captains; a two-page version was sent to a randomly selected sample of city residents. The short police survey was also put in city libraries and city halls so that any citizen could anonymously voice his or her opinion. It was available for approximately one month. To prevent citizens from submitting multiple surveys, each one was numbered. The survey did not ask for demographic variables, and was specifically for citizens in the targeted areas rather than business owners. All information from the various police surveys was consolidated by the SPD, and the results are listed below:

- The department found that the most serious crime problems were drugs, burglary and theft, assault and violent crimes, and gangs.
- Citizen satisfaction was highest with the 911 telephone system and operator assistance.
- Citizens rated the Seattle Police Department and its effectiveness in stopping crime in the following manner:
  —Patrolling in cars
  —Community organizing/Block Watch Program
  —Bicycle patrols
  —Foot patrols
  —Community police teams

—Education in schools
- Citizen satisfaction was lowest with Seattle Police Department's response to non-emergency calls, detective follow-up, and dealing with crime in general.
- Respondents from the West and North Precincts were most satisfied with police services in general, while the respondents from the South and East Precincts were the least satisfied.
- About two-thirds of the citizens (69 percent of 365 people) responding to the long form survey indicated that more than the existing four precinct stations are needed.
- Eighty-three percent of the respondents to the long survey, which had a 26 percent overall response rate, favored a separate seven-digit telephone number for non-emergency calls to the police department.
- Overall, about 88 percent of the 26 percent responding were supportive of the Seattle Police Department and/or wanted more services. About 12 percent indicated that the Seattle Police Department was the problem. As an organization, it was deemed irresponsible and non-supportive of citizens' concerns.
- About 12 percent (69 people) of the 26 percent responding to the long form survey indicated that they wanted to file a complaint about the Seattle Police Department. Of this 12 percent, 32 percent actually filed a complaint, and 50 percent were satisfied with how the complaint was handled. Sixty-two percent wanted more information about the Seattle Police Department's formal complaint process.

The politics of police-conducted surveys were found by the researcher to be subtly tied to the urban political processes in the city. For instance, the Seattle Police Department constantly focused on the serious violent crime problem in Seattle. However, a cursory look at the SPD's crime data (1985-1993) showed there was relative stability in the crime rate. The murder rate did not reach an all-time high until 1993, and that rate in itself is low by national standards. The SPD's public relations materials constantly focuses on violent crime, gang problems, repeat career offenders, and crimes by youth.

What is not being stressed in the material is that the Seattle Police Department is responsible for protecting the image of the city and controlling street crime. What is of most concern to the SPD is the

quality of life issues for those people coming to the city to spend
money and live in the northwest corner of the United States.

In this researcher's opinion, it appeared that the police chief's
concern was with shaping community policing externally and its
implementation in the Seattle Police Department internally. The public
relations materials revealed that the SPD thought there would be more
demand for the police to assist with quality of life types of problems,
such as graffiti clean-up, abandoned buildings, street lighting, and other
neighborhood issues. Subtly, the political and economic issues became
clear: middle-class consumers would be pressuring the city to maintain
its historical quality of life. In the end, the chief felt that a token form of
community policing would satisfy the public, and he would not have to
face going back to the city council and the mayor for more monies.

Public Documents and Interviews

Two questions posed by the researcher to police officials, community-
based leaders, and neighborhood activists were: (1) In what ways does
community policing reduce crime in Seattle? (2) What are the forces
that led to community policing in Seattle? These questions are
important because they help one understand why the Seattle Police
Department implemented community policing and what diverse groups
felt about the new initiative.

A position paper written by James Scott, Executive Director of the
Washington State Criminal Justice Training Commission, explains
organizationally why the Seattle Police Department pursued
community policing in Seattle (unpublished paper, 1990). He indicates:

> The methods and tactics that are currently being used to combat crime
> are clearly not working. There will never be enough resources to
> adequately respond to crime in this manner. Community Policing,
> policing that focuses upon prevention of crime, is the only strategy that
> has proven successful in the era of static, and dwindling, resources.
> Furthermore, Community Policing is probably the most effective way
> of fighting our two most pressing crime problems, drug abuse and
> gang violence.

Scott proceeds to outline how the philosophy of community policing
would change the deployment techniques and tactics in neighborhoods
and communities around the city. It would also change the recruitment

and training of officers, by hiring more service-oriented individuals. The administrative chain of command would be open, flexible, and have fewer officers in the chain. Police officers would be called upon to work in proactive teams rather than as individuals reacting to criminal incidents. He intimates that there would always be a problem finding enough resources to respond to crime, and that therefore community policing offers the best approach to dealing with street crime in Seattle.

The community policing teams in Seattle became the test for future crime control and crime-prevention endeavors. Specifically, the community policing teams implemented in 1990 were supervised by a sergeant who reported to the operational lieutenant who was under a precinct commander. The structure was governed by the normal chain of command. Community policing teams were composed of officers from other units and precincts who volunteered for the new assignment. No new resources were used for this new deployment effort. It is important to note that the patrol division was not involved directly in the community policing deployment strategy. However, the community policing team officers worked closely with the patrol division regarding street crime.

Community Policing and Crime Reduction

Regarding whether community policing reduced crime in Seattle, respondents to the author's research questionnaire indicated the following:

- "Community policing does not reduce crime, it just displaces it" (neighborhood activist, H.W.).
- "Community policing as crime prevention does work" (neighborhood activist, G.D.).
- "Community policing actually reduces crime block to block. Community policing in a small, concentrated area works" (neighborhood activist, K.O.).
- "Community policing means being proactive and present" (neighborhood activist, C.A.).
- "Community policing does not reduce crime in the inner city. The process has not been to reduce crime, and arrests are basically symbolic" (neighborhood activist, C.J.).
- "Community policing can stay on top of criminal activity somewhat" (neighborhood activist, R.T.).

- "Community policing closed down drug houses, and drug dealing became more sophisticated" (neighborhood activist, M.E.B.).
- "Unsure if community policing is having an impact on crime" (neighborhood activist, L.G.).
- "Community policing reduced the intensity of crime" (neighborhood activist, R.S.).
- "Community policing caused crime rate to go down. Community support and cooperation evidenced" (SSCPC leader, N.C.).
- "Police visibility will depress crime. Some evidence exists that a small group of police have developed linkages and relationships with young people. These young people respect the police" (educator, W.H.).
- "Community policing reduces crime where the police are known and visible" (judge, J.H.).
- "Community policing is not designed to reduce crime. It is designed to reduce the fear of crime. The goal is to reduce crime" (chief of police).
- "Community policing displaces crime" (lieutenant, East Precinct).
- "Community policing reduces crime by getting the community involved, e.g., drug houses, clue lines, and removal of abandoned cars" (sergeant, South Precinct).
- "Community policing reduces crime by giving alternatives to criminal activity and improving communications with youth" (sergeant, East Precinct).
- "Community policing reduced crime in Seattle by more crime prevention and solution of crime problems with the help of citizens" (police official).

The above statements were given as responses to the author's questionnaire regarding community policing. As indicated, eight of the respondents argued that community policing reduced crime, while six respondents said that community policing does not reduce crime. One individual was neutral, and one was unsure if community policing was having an impact regarding crime reduction. Neighborhood activists' responses were less technical, while police officials talked about the importance of community residents becoming involved in partnerships with the police department. For instance, one police official's views seemed to reflect the department's official position regarding community policing. Several residents seemed to be supportive of the small community policing teams, and some indicated a desire for more community policing teams to get involved in crime reduction activities.

Forces Leading to Community Policing

According to respondents to the researcher's questionnaire, the forces that led to this community policing configuration in the Seattle Police Department were the following:

- "South end crime-prevention council pushed the police department, and the police department saw a value in the new efforts" (city official, J.D.).
- "South Seattle Crime Prevention Council and the police department developed a 15-Point Plan, the result of which was the community policing teams" (chief of police).
- "Demand from the community for better community-police relations" (sergeant, East Precinct).
- "Escalating cost of traditional policing. Law enforcement was emerging as less a part of the community" (educator, W.H.).
- "Complaints from residents and businesses about crime and drug dealing" (neighborhood activist, R.T.).
- "Community policing configuration was born out of a desire of the mayor to improve the relations between inner city African-Americans and the police" (neighborhood activist, L.G.).
- "Articles in the *Seattle Times* by the City of Bellevue [neighboring suburb] Police Chief" (neighborhood activist, G.D.).
- "Fashion/style. It was the thing to do" (neighborhood activist, K.O.).
- "Community pressure" (SSCPC leader, N.C.).
- "Community pushing for something 'different' and 'new'" (neighborhood activist, R.S.).

Again, the above responses were given on the author's research questionnaire. According to respondents, the main forces that led to this configuration were the South Seattle Crime Prevention Council and community pressure. The media were also mentioned as an influence by one respondent. Overall, the responses were less varied. These responses are important because they help illustrate how the Seattle

Police Department maneuvered through internal and external pressures to implement a model of community policing.

LOCAL COMMUNITY AND HUMAN AGENCY

As explained earlier, south end and central district citizens organized to put political pressure on the Seattle Police Department to do something about crime during the period 1985-1993. Information from public documents, books, and interviews seems to verify that a miniature social movement for change in the police department took place. First, residents were fed up with street crime in the central district and the south end. Second, residents organized and put pressure on elected political officials to take seriously their local crime problem. Third, the Weed & Seed program to be implemented in the central district as a bridge to community policing created controversy and was viewed with apprehension by the local community. Evidence indicates that residents compromised and negotiated with the mayor's office, city council people, and the police chief around both community policing and the Weed & Seed program.

Scheingold (1990) wrote extensively about the politicization of street crime in Seattle. He argues that residents in the central district and the south end disagreed about the strategies that would resolve street crime. For instance, south end leaders were able to frame their response to crime as part of the powerful law and order movement of the 1970s, and to influence the Seattle Police Department to adopt community policing and its implementation. By contrast, the central district leaders and residents were disorganized and unable to offer politically acceptable short or long-term solutions to the street crime problem.

Several community-based groups in both districts were interviewed, and they were split in their support of community policing. For instance, the Garfield Community Council (located in the heart of the central district) was pro-community policing. The Garfield Community Council leadership was supportive of the chief of police and the police department. They felt that the department would seriously consider the problems they nominated for police intervention in their area. In contrast, the Mothers Against Police Harassment (a non-profit central district organization formed to help change the unresolved issues of police accountability) were anti-community policing. The leaders of this group acted to resolve their own problems without police support. They felt that if community policing was implemented in their area, they would lose control. Many residents of the central district saw the police department as the problem, and indicated that the police department needed to change and weed out its own bad apples. Consequently, they wanted no part of the mayor's proposals for crime prevention or control. Some vocal residents wanted to get rid of the chief and bring in someone who was accountable and sympathetic to their views about policing and crime reduction. The movement for social change is defined herein as the politics of community policing in Seattle.

The mayor's office, the city council, and the Seattle Police Department responded symbolically to the street crime problem in Seattle. In the introduction to Murray Edelman's book, *Political Language* (1977:xviii), Michael Lipsky helps the reader understand political symbolism:

> The pluralistic aspects of American politics, through opportunities for individual, direct participation in politics and through group affiliations, might seem at first glance to provide people with the chance to affect political life. Yet careful analysis of pluralist assumptions over the past ten years reveals that pluralism does not substantially contradict the proposition that American politics manipulates mass attitudes and perspectives. Pluralism may ensure competition among elites and at times may provide masses with opportunities to participate in decision making, thus conveying a sense that popular democracy thrives. But pluralism in practice also means elite dominion on the major issues salient to elites, severe limitations on protest group activity, and manipulation of the terms on which issues arise and are processed.

Lipsky's analysis of pluralism is particularly relevant for analyzing the limitations and opportunities of grassroots mobilization against crime in Seattle, particularly the development of community policing. Organized political elites in Seattle responded in a way that protected downtown business interests, the integrity of the city council, and the legitimation of the Seattle Police Department. At first glance, it seems that pluralism explains how the political process handled the diverse number of complaints regarding street crime. However, the chief ended up co-opting, compromising, and negotiating out demands from the

SSCPC and central district activists' demands to do something about street crime.

The interviews conducted by this author illustrate that the SSCPC was able to convince the mayor's office, city council, and the police chief to enter into a 15-Point Plan to resolve street crime on the south end. The researcher believes that the 15-Point Plan was watered down and flawed and acted chiefly to provide a sophisticated buffer between the police department and the community.

However, the disorganized and vocal anti-Weed & Seed activists in the central district were also able to subtly influence the mayor's office, the city council, and the police chief. They did not have the long-term staying power to overturn the application and implementation of Weed & Seed.

Public officials in Seattle have both public and private agendas regarding social change, as most politicians do. At the top of the agenda is how best to manage the urban crime problem. Interviews conducted showed that where one situates oneself on the political scale explains a lot about one's perspective on political issues and problem-solving solutions. For example, employees of the police department supported and used the organizational rhetoric and language of community policing and Weed & Seed. Neighborhood activists who criticized the police department neither used this organizational rhetoric nor supported the police department's application of community policing and Weed & Seed. They disagreed about the approach to solving the crime and drug problems and the utilization of the community policing teams and federal Weed & Seed funds. For instance, one African-American male community leader was anti-police and anti-community policing. He indicated that police were used to contain the inner city community but were guardians in the white community and suburbs.

A viewpoint from inside the police department was that community policing and Weed & Seed programs were welcome changes to fight street crime and drug trafficking. Residents of the central district who were critical of the Weed & Seed program indicated that the "neighborhoods desperately needed funding, but the way to go is not through Weed & Seed" (personal communication, 1993). Another resident indicated, "We need police accountability in the central district, not Weed & Seed" (personal communication, 1993). Another resident said, "Council people who support Weed & Seed will be weeded out come next election" (personal communication, 1993).

Several stated, "We need a new mayor and a new city council who have a new vision" (personal communication, 1993).

Media Influence

W. Lance Bennett (1983), a Seattle resident and professor in the political science department at the University of Washington, notes that the news takes us on a daily tour of a world filled with comforting images of authority and security. In Seattle, the local mass media helped frame and construct the discussion about crime, community policing, and the debate around Weed & Seed. Local newspaper columnists and editors subtly helped set the agenda regarding the local crime problem. According to one source interviewed, the mayor, the city council, and the police chief had a cozy relationship with the newspapers and were not criticized personally in print about crime issues (personal communication, 1993). Bennett (1983) indicates that local news seems to splinter into one or more of the following categories: reports of law-breaking, violence, or distasteful behavior that tends to discredit the actors involved; reports that balance a deviant perspective with an official reaction in opposition; and reports of the positive activities of groups that quickly fade from the news, implying that the group and its goals are of little value.

There are exceptions to Bennett's point of view, however. For example, the *Seattle Times* (August 9, 1991:A8) editor noted that a police shooting of a handcuffed and fleeing felon raised troublesome questions. The editor raised an important question: Should the Seattle Police Department allow an officer to shoot a fleeing, unarmed, handcuffed felony suspect in the back if no threat is present? The editorial argued that the answer is no and stated:

> On the surface, that appears to be what happened when Officer Larry Cotton shot an escaping felony suspect, Gregory R. Jones, 30, of Richmond Beach, in the back Tuesday. Jones was stopped for a minor traffic violation, then ran from police into a Ballard auto firm, where he threw tools at officers and fought with them. Warrants were out for his arrest, including one for robbery. He was taken to Harborview for treatment, then ran from police as he was being taken from the hospital to jail. That's when he was shot. . . . Jones had his hands cuffed in front of him and tried to commandeer a van, but the driver kept him out.

This *Seattle Times* editorial argued that police policy requires "the use of every reasonable means to capture a fleeing felon before using force that could cause death or serious injury. Yet, Treadwell said it appears guidelines were followed." Seattle city policy, which mirrors that of the state, allows officers to use deadly force to defend themselves or others in danger or to prevent the escape of a felon.

In this case, the newspaper editorial questioned the Seattle city policy on the use of deadly force and indicated that it must be more clear and concise and should be predicated on the existence of danger to officers or others. Finally, the editor stated that if the present policy does not make that clear, either department training or a revision of the policy is needed.

This example illustrates that there are both limitations and opportunities for citizen mobilization against city hall. The residents of the south end succeeded in getting the mayor's office, the city council, and the police department to take them seriously on one or two issues regarding street crime and community policing. However, the residents of the central district, who were poor, powerless, and vocal, were unable to gain allies in the mayor's office, city council, or police department.

COMMUNITY POLICING AS THE SOLUTION

Fleissner et al. (1992) describe community policing in Seattle as a model partnership between citizens and police. This chapter examined political, management, fiscal crisis, and pressures in the city during the period when community policing teams were created in January 1990. This topic covered urban political issues, as well as micro-organizational implications, which must be discussed together because theoretically the two overlap. The author also looked for evidence that the Seattle government (police, city council, and mayor's office) established buffers to enhance their image in the eyes of the general public or with specific segments.

Community policing was a political response offered by the mayor's office, city council, and the police department as a solution to the crime problem in Seattle. In reality, only 30 officers out of a total of 1,200 were organized into community policing teams. These teams were involved in public relations and problem-solving-type activities that started in the south end and were eventually replicated in the other three precincts. In other words, there was one community policing officer for every 16,666 residents in the city—-at best a limited partnership in the overall context of Seattle policing. No plan was uncovered to evaluate the effectiveness of community policing, and no financial commitment was made to the transition from traditional policing to this token form of community policing. However, research shows that the public safety budget climbed from around 186 million to approximately 213 million between 1985 and 1993.

Community policing was offered as a panacea and a solution to the crime problem. It was symbolic in nature, and no real commitment was made on the part of the government to flatten out the police organization or become more responsive to neighborhood and community needs.

News accounts and interviews showed that the police chief had an ongoing feud with ministers and local central district leaders (*Seattle Times*, February 13, 1994:B1). The chief had gained and maintained some legitimacy in the local community by joining the local Catholic church 15 years earlier. He is credited with stamping out corruption in the police department and adding a sense of professionalism, according to local leaders and the leading newspapers in the city.

The author argues that although crime rates did decrease, community policing cannot be the sole reason for this success as proponents claim. Fleissner et al. (1992:10) state, "Calls for service rose sharply throughout Seattle from 1984 onward. While they declined slightly beginning in 1988 for other parts of the city, in the south they continued to rise." They continue, "This trend may reflect a rise in public awareness of police services following the formation of the South Seattle Crime Prevention Council." The best evidence seems to show that crime was displaced, neighborhood residents got more involved, and, most of all, arrests and convictions were up and offenders were taken off the streets in record numbers (Seattle District Attorney's Office Annual Report, 1993).

Seattle officials enjoyed support in the north end and west end communities of Seattle. However, those same officials lacked the trust and confidence of their constituents in pockets of the central district and south end communities. The police chief was faced with the near-impossible task of balancing responding to crime with political pressures. In the *Seattle Times* (February 13, 1994:B1), a reporter noted that Chief Fitzsimons had soured relationships with minority communities during his 15-year tenure.

The support for the chief and the department in the south end and central district was fragile and elusive because of the socioeconomic status of those areas. Public project dwellers and renters were not as supportive as were homeowners in stable neighborhoods. The south end and central district were dominated by three large public housing projects (Holly Park, Rainier Vista, Yesler Terrace). The Seattle Police Department's largest numbers of calls for services were from low-income communities in the south end and central district (Seattle Police Department annual reports, 1985-1993). These are the areas that provided the most problems for the mayor, city council, and police chief. These actors felt that it was important image-wise and symbolically to do something about street crime in those neighborhoods and communities.

Buffers

In Seattle, a number of buffers were set up either consciously or unconsciously to keep and maintain distance between the police department and the local community. Buffers may be conceptualized as social-control apparatuses of the society and as an interlocking set of coercive symbolic and institutional processes that soften the impact of basic social contradictions and that induce or compel people to act against their interests, often by not acting at all (Katznelson, 1976).

The external buffers operating in Seattle were the SSCPC, neighborhood groups, and community councils. The internal organizational buffers were the gang units of the police department, the add-on units, the police internal auditor, and the community policing teams.

Katznelson (1976:220) indicates that stability in a capitalist political economy does not imply the absence of structurally rooted conflicts. He implies that stability reflects the operation of the buffering mechanisms that shape and limit behavior. He goes on to say:

> The state's function of social control consists in managing the consequences of making capitalism work and can best be understood as an attempt to manage but not overcome the contradictions of the capitalist system.

Katznelson's (1976) theory of buffers helps explain the urban political processes in Seattle. He states, and this author concurs, that the two most important sets of political buffers are symbolic and institutional. Community policing in Seattle during the period under study is best described as "the velvet glove" of policing (Criminal and Social Justice Associates, 1994). Community policing in its token form has hidden and subtle ideological values.

At the heart of the urban political processes model is the understanding of how legitimacy plays a role in government. High levels of legitimacy indicate successful social control. Moreover, it is social control at the least cost to rulers (Lipset, 1963). However, legitimacy of the dominant hegemonic value system is difficult to measure in a democratic society. Political scientists have traditionally tried to measure legitimacy by looking at the number of citizens who vote. An alternative measure might be to look at the level of support for programs and activities purported to solve local problems such as street crime.

This research showed that for community policing-type programs to be effective at reducing crime, they must be integrated into the neighborhoods in which they are functioning. This implies that the neighborhood must be organizationally prepared to participate in the functioning of these mechanisms and they must ultimately function to strengthen the neighborhood unit, to work with the systems of informal social control and integration and not to further disrupt or disorganize the neighborhood unit (Iadicola, 1988).

Buffers do not empower neighborhood groups to get involved in solving their own crime problems. They set up and continue the us versus them philosophy as cultivated by the Seattle Police Department. The department appeared to master the buffer technology as illustrated and depicted by Katznelson (1976). Iadicola (1988) presents an opposing theory, arguing that the fundamental features of true empowerment efforts are to address community-based problems. He asserts that the neighborhood must play an active role in policing itself and directing the efforts of formal police forces, but also handle disputes internally through mediation, as well as play a role in the correcting of perpetrators and the damage they have done to the community. The left realism theory offered by Iadicola (1988) is the opposite of what happened in Seattle during the period under study. Community policing in Seattle was not an illustration of true empowerment efforts. The community policing team members were able to organize citizens and resolve conflict on a small scale, not community-wide.

Urban political processes help to analyze and illuminate the development of a token form of community policing in Seattle. There were competing centers of power and authority in Seattle. The chief of police in Seattle understood the competing centers of power, and that power rested in his hands. The chief was not interested the sharing of power, and wanted to control the department with an iron fist. He saw police chiefs come and go during his 30-year tenure in law enforcement, and did not want to share law enforcement power with non-experts. From his perspective, the police were the experts. The chief cleaned the department of corruption and established a good relationship with the media. He was not going to change his traditional department overnight to satisfy a few "rabble-rousers" in the local community, especially the "central area radicals" who wanted to influence the running of his department.

Community policing experts suggest that police departments be open to problems nominated by the community. The chief of the SPD was not willing to be open-armed and all-embracing of concerns of all residents. He felt a need to control potentially volatile situations in the central district and in the south end. Consequently, this caused the emergence of buffers in every precinct of the city. The department was alert to the appropriation of federal money for crime and gang prevention programs.

Not all residents were critical of the chief's management style. For instance, some segments of the public were both proactive and reactive in their support of the police department. The chief understood those elements very well and fashioned a form of policing that would be appropriate to each precinct and neighborhood. City government officials responded with community policing to improve its image and legitimation in high-crime areas in consultation with the chief and major advisors.

Citizens' organization and human agency were quite fluid in Seattle, and influenced all of the actors to do something about street crime. Citizens organized and put pressure on city council members, the mayor, and the police chief around street crime and public disorder. The token form of community policing helped all of these actors buy time in reference to the local street crime problem. No attempt was made to solve the deep-seated structural problems in Seattle. Grassroots leaders were fully aware of the pitfalls of the small token community policing teams. On the one hand, politicians understood the price they pay for being perceived as going soft on crime. On the other hand, politicians in Seattle did not want to be perceived as callous and mean-spirited toward street-level crime, dealers, and gun violence.

The buffers provided the opportunity for some individuals to take the blame rather than the government officials shouldering the responsibility and risking re-election. An example of a buffer was the appointment of former Judge Terrence Carroll to deal with internal investigations and allegations of police force and brutality. In his 1993 reports, the judge acted as a liaison for the police department and the community, by indicating that unnecessary force allegations in 1992 were prevalent but not epidemic.

The ex-judge recommended some minor changes in the police department internally. He suggested that as the Seattle Police Department does not require applicants to possess a college education, it should do so because not having a college education impaired the individual officer. He suggested that the discipline process should be streamlined, more accountable, and more open. However, he noted that there was no need for civilian review of the police. He cited literature to show that civilian review boards did not increase the likelihood of an officer being disciplined. He emphasized that lay persons not familiar with police work are not necessarily in a good position to determine whether a department's policy was violated. Finally, he wanted the public to know that the appointment of persons to a civilian review board normally would be made in part for political purposes, not for talent or expertise.

The department faced both internal and external political pressures to implement community policing, buffers, and consultive committees, because these were:

> not just a government and police smokescreen or public relations exercise. It is not just *against* accountability—it is *for* the co-optation of the community into policing. (Gordon, 1987:136)

An August 1993 calendar illustrates the above point by documenting regular meetings of the police-community relations task force. These groups were composed of civilian city employees, police officers, and special interest leaders. Minutes of the meetings show that the police voices dominated these task force meetings and were forums for the police chief to speak to specialized groups in the International District, the Greater Seattle Business Association, the Queer Nation, and the Privacy Fund. The author was informed by a staff member of the city council Public Safety Committee that the purpose of these meetings was to maintain constant relationships with diverse groups around the city. An ongoing example of buffers organized and orchestrated by the Seattle Police Department was the development of police-community relations task forces citywide.

A series of urban political processes is at work when dealing with street crime, community policing, and Weed & Seed-type programs; and the mayor's office, the city council, and the police department are all involved in the dynamics of these public policies. It should be noted that there is conflict and cooperation among and within these political actors' organizations and bureaucracies. These relationships are both fluid and conflictual, based on the issues and stakes. Each is jockeying for political power, support, and legitimacy from its constituents.

The next chapter analyzes how micro-organizational characteristics affected the political process and the formation of the token community policing teams. The police chief's 15-year tenure had both positive and negative aspects. The positive attributes were that he cleaned up corruption that had existed dating from the 1950s, he got along well with the mainstream media, and he was pro-management. The negative attributes were that he conflicted with elected officials and city council staff, and had generally poor relationships with active inner city community groups.

CHAPTER 5

Micro-Organizational Processes

This chapter analyzes how police organizations address social problems and adapt to changing demands from diverse constituents. This level of analysis is based on Bouza's (1990:47) theory that "any organization's relations with the outside world are shaped by what's going on internally." To that end, we must examine how micro-organizational characteristics shaped the political process and community policing in Seattle. Net widening often indicates the police organization's willingness to grow and expand its organizational control mechanisms. The chief of police and high-level bureaucrats resisted the organizational flattening and the increased accountability to diverse communities required by community policing experts. Members of the department were supportive of community policing philosophies that protected the existing organizational structure and were critical of other arrangements that threatened its hegemony.

The meaning of community policing to the Seattle Police Department's bureaucrats and street-level officers was explored. The ways in which external pressures on the department to do something about street crime impacted the organization *internally* were scrutinized, along with street crime problems and blue uniform policing in Seattle. Organizational add-ons, discussed generally in the previous chapters, are now critiqued for their impact on micro-organizational processes. Interviews were conducted, and internal police memos and documents and city and community newspapers were gathered regarding community policing efforts in Seattle.

Factors that might have led the Seattle Police Department to adopt a form of community policing in the two precincts are highlighted. This research found the *internal* characteristics and/or pressures on the

Seattle Police Department to be auditors and consultants, proactive deployment strategies, community policing advocates, internal affairs and investigation, and middle management. There are two questions that will help the reader understand the police organization and the micro-organizational processes in Seattle: (1) What did community policing mean to the police department in Seattle? (2) How did *external* pressures to do something about street crime affect the Seattle Police Department *internally*?

BLUE UNIFORM POLICING
AND MICRO-ORGANIZATIONAL PROCESSES

"Blue uniform" policing, as defined by Brogden, Jefferson, and Walklate (1988), helps define and illustrate the researcher's theory of the events in Seattle in 1985-1993. Brogden et al. suggest that policing or state work implies a range of functions, namely enforcing and sometimes defining the criminal law, maintaining order, gathering intelligence, and securing consent—all directed toward a singular end: upholding the general legal framework of the state. These authors argue that police work in a postmodern society involves securing and maintaining consent or ideological control in order to facilitate the reproduction of order in society. Subtly, police organizations define the criminal law, maintain order, and gather intelligence in local communities. These police tactics are not obvious to the general public and non-law enforcement individuals. Thus, the nature of blue uniform policing in postmodern society is highly complex and sophisticated.

Organization and Bureaucratic Structure

The police organization is a social organization that has an internal and external culture, behavior, and dynamics. To illustrate this point, former police chief Bouza (1990:48) reminds us that any organization's relations with the outside world are shaped by what's going on internally. From his 30 years of experience, Bouza alleges:

> Organizational messages are transmitted most eloquently through actions rather than through the most pious memos or fervent orders. Members check to see what gets done and how it is accomplished, and then they respond accordingly. Cops will translate organizational messages into situationally relevant symbols. They will adapt their

behavior to conform with what's expected or permitted and will avoid what is rejected.

Radelet (1986) indicates that a bureaucracy is a system of administration characterized by specialization of functions, adherence to fixed rules, and a hierarchy of authority. Radelet says that historically the more bureaucratic the organization was, the more professional it was deemed to be. The Seattle Police Department was a traditional bureaucratic structured organization that resisted the changes required by community policing experts.

Manning (1988:31) describes the two types of policing envisioned by both police and police researchers: bureaucratic type and community policing type.

> The bureaucratic police are focused on crime as a legal infraction and are disinterested in "community work" as not truly "police work." The community policing type is peopled by visible, available, and personal officers. The officers, often located in a neighborhood school, storefront, or ministation when not out serving the public on foot, represent a form of dedifferentiated social control. . . . The officer represents a kind of symbol for the community and stands in contrast to the stereotypic crime-focused specialist.

Both types of officers appear in the Seattle Police Department as the agency maneuvered through political pressures between 1985 and 1993 to create what community policing supporters claim is a model program. The majority of officers in the SPD were the bureaucratic type, and resisted community policing philosophical and structural changes. A small number of community policing team officers were willing to accept and implement the basic theories and philosophies of community policing in the central district and south end.

Benveniste (1983) insists that scholars understand the relations between people in positions of authority and their minions. One needs to understand how organizations (both internally and externally) influence and control the behavior of citizens. The public must distinguish between what the social organization claims, and what they can infer about reality. Postmodern people are at the mercy of social organizations (Benveniste, 1983).

Lipsky (1980) notes that street-level bureaucrats make policy by exercising wide discretion in decisions about citizens. Lipsky's comment reflects the development of community policing in the Seattle Police Department. According to an officer who was interviewed, the community policing officer has the authority and the latitude to use his own discretion when responding to 911 calls, to re-establish face-to-face relations with the community, and to prevent crimes rather than just react when they happen.

MEANING OF COMMUNITY POLICING IN SEATTLE

Several definitions of community policing were offered by police officials and street-level officers in Seattle. The diversity of definitions offered by these actors may be explained by the individual's own perception of the concept and philosophy of community policing. The individuals at the top of the bureaucracy understood the academic definitions, as well as the street-level reality of the concept. Many street-level officers felt that community policing meant social work and non-law enforcement type duties and responsibilities. As discussed earlier, the philosophy of community policing contains critical assumptions and ideologies about the nature of police departments.

Riechers and Roberg (1990) discuss several critical assumptions related to community policing, including the assumption that paramilitary police organizations can readily adapt to a more flexible structure and managerial style. They question whether police organizations could implement a true version of community policing given their present structure and organization. Writing three years later, Kennedy (1993) also warns that the individual initiative which community policing demands cannot be combined with the paramilitary hierarchy. The hierarchy of a police department needs to be considered when reviewing the responses of the Seattle Police Department, a traditional bureaucratic organization, to the implementation of community policing. Upper- and middle management of the SPD failed to adapt to the structural changes required to implement community policing programs as advanced by experts and advocates.

Seattle Police Department Police Agency Dynamics

To understand the police agency, one must look at its organizational configuration. Fleissner et al. (1991) state that there are two broad issues concerning the organizational configuration of police agencies in the community policing model: (1) deployment, and (2) command and control. Concerning the deployment (geography and human resources) of personnel, the authors contend that four possible organizational configurations could be derived: (1) department-wide with all officers involved, (2) department-wide with specialist community officers, (3) community officers in some geographical subsections of a department, (4) specialist community officers in some geographical subsections of a department.

It appears that the Seattle Police Department followed the fourth type of organizational configuration of community policing delineated by Fleissner et al. (1991). Between 1985 and 1993 the Seattle Police Department implemented a variety of community policing-type programs and crime-prevention and crime control activities. Activities adopted during this time period were the mountain bike patrol, anti-crime unit, gang unit, neighborhood and block watches, Seattle Teen for Youth, and the community policing teams. The community policing teams were specialist community officers (twelve or fewer officers in each precinct) doing community policing in each of the four precincts in Seattle. Basically, training was limited, policing took place eight hours a day, rather than 24 hours, and there appeared to be no community policing evaluation mechanism. In addition, no effort was made to implement community policing department-wide. Fleissner et al. (1991) noted that specialist officers create problems because they are dependent on their generalist peers for much of the information required to engage in successful community problem-solving. Furthermore, the advent of specialist units commonly leads to less efficient communication within an organization.

The second issue concerning organizational configuration is command and control. According to Fleissner et al. (1991) organizational flexibility is a requirement so that police services can be tailored to the specific needs of individual communities. Police departments are directed to decentralize operations to the neighborhood level, assigning officers on a permanent basis to given neighborhoods and then placing them in charge of problem-solving in their neighborhoods. Fleissner et al. (1991) note that the nature of community problems should guide deployment practices rather than a given organizational philosophy. This viewpoint was widespread within the Seattle Police Department (Fleissner et al., 1991).

One method of internal control in the SPD was to articulate a perspective of uniqueness and expertise within their organization. Most important, top level officials worked hard to placate an overly demanding and critical segment of the community intent on exercising control over the police operations (Goldstein, 1993). For instance, the department resisted using sergeants and lieutenants to assist the beat cop with his or her efforts to solve community problems. It fought against any form of decentralization of command and control strategies. Also, the department fought against institutionalized police accountability to central district residents. However, it embraced the SSCPC's activities in the south end by entering into the 15-Point Plan with the SSCPC (Appendix B).

Police Interviews

During the summer of 1993, several police officers and officials were interviewed by this author regarding the community policing program in Seattle. The interviews were informative and revealed the internal dynamics of the community policing teams and the Seattle Police Department between 1985 and 1993.

The first question asked during the interviews was, What does community policing mean to the Seattle Police Department? A sergeant in the community policing team unit in the East Precinct indicated that it means empowering residents and improving police-community relations. He also indicated that community policing is proactive policing, which to him means "getting to know people in the community," including both law-abiding citizens and criminals. When asked if he thought community policing reduced fear of crime, he felt that it made people feel safer. In his precinct, he believed community policing provides alternatives to criminal activities. He felt that it helps police become more service-oriented and breaks down barriers and stereotypes (personal interview, 1993).

Another sergeant said that community policing is about getting the public involved and working closely with crime prevention. It means preventing community problems and having community policing teams spend time in schools meeting young people. This sergeant also believed that community policing breaks down barriers between the police and the community (personal interview, 1993).

A lieutenant in the East Precinct said that community policing means working as a team to solve problems. The lieutenant described community policing as a crime control strategy. He felt that community policing merely displaces crime. He also said that old traditional policing does not work (personal interview, 1993).

A police official in the planning unit indicated that community policing means a partnership with businesses and communities, and combining communication and problem-solving. He felt that community policing is a way to improve the provision of public safety services and to help solve neighborhood decay and urban blight problems (personal interview, 1993).

The police chief said that community policing in Seattle was a reaction to the failures of the criminal justice system, and that it was not a new concept. To him, it means police taking a lead regarding community safety, total equality policing, and freedom for police to do other things. Furthermore, it means enlisting citizens to support the police and to get citizens to solve their own problems (personal interview, 1993).

From the five police officials and street-level officers interviewed, it was learned that the police chief was suspicious of a full-blown version of community policing for Seattle. He intimated that neighborhood-oriented policing (NOP) means "nobody on patrol." Another official in the planning unit said that community policing in Seattle was best illustrated by police meeting with citizens and being open to their requests, needs, and priorities. These two police officials gave bureaucratic responses and spoke the jargon of policing. The lieutenant and two sergeants felt that community policing was a way to improve service delivery and improve internal and external communication. These officers were closer to the local community than the two top officials and seemed to be enthusiastic about the strong relationships and cooperation they were gaining from residents. Taken all together, the interviews revealed diverse responses to the goals of Seattle's community policing effort.

SSCPC AND THE DEVELOPMENT OF NEW LAWS

To understand how the Seattle Police Department maneuvered to implement a version of community policing, it must be made clear that the South Seattle Crime Prevention Council was an organized external force which impacted the Seattle Police Department internally. They were able to gain the confidence of high-level officials. The officials, in turn, wanted concessions from the SSCPC. The police gave the SSCPC public legitimacy and support for their grievances about street crime in south Seattle. In exchange, the SSCPC supplied individuals who went to the city council and the state capital (Olympia) to lobby for a range of law enforcement policies, such as search warrant and abatement laws, civil abatement process laws, drug loitering laws, and drug-free zones. (The author gained this knowledge by talking to various individuals in the police department and community groups in Seattle.)

The SSCPC (a.k.a. the Rainier Chamber of Commerce) worked closely with the Seattle Police Department during the early 1990s to fashion a nuisance abatement ordinance. This ordinance was passed in August 1992. It gave the city authority to declare what shall be a public nuisance; to impose fines upon parties who may create, continue, or allow public nuisances to exist; and to prescribe solutions to decrease the public nuisances. The purpose of this law was to come down on the pervasive problem of street violence, noise, public drunkenness, drug trafficking, and other illegal activities that endangered the health, comfort, and safety of the community that were, in part, the result of properties that attract and encourage such behavior. Criminals who created an unsafe environment became of such magnitude that they were a concern to the city. This law was citywide but primarily targeted and extended social control mechanisms in the south end and central district.

During the period 1985-1993, the SSCPC worked closely with the Seattle Police Department to construct and pass laws that extended the net of social control as the department was championing community policing. The SSCPC stressed that it supported the public's desire to fight drugs, drug trafficking, and street gangs. This law provided the chief with another weapon in the war against street crime and criminals. Specifically, this law was administered and enforced by the chief of police, although other city departments and divisions were authorized to assist.

The selective application of these laws by the police department seemed to disproportionately target minorities and blacks in the south end and central district. This systematic discrimination appears to widen the net of social control, as reflected by the high number of arrests, convictions, and incarcerations of minorities from these two districts in comparison with the rest of the districts in the city.

The war against drugs and street crime often pits the grim realities of the streets against stubborn racial and class stereotypes. Blacks and minorities are arrested, stopped and questioned, and shot and killed by the police out of proportion to their representation in the population (Walker et al., 1996). Chambliss (1994) argues that blacks and the poor are the scapegoats for the war on drugs and increased budgets for law enforcement nationwide. According to Chambliss, African-Americans have very little political clout, few resources to defend themselves successfully against criminal charges, and a public image as a group in which crime is endemic. Free (1996) states that blacks represent 12.1 percent of the population of the United States (approximately 30 million), but they account for 28.9 percent of those arrested. Therefore, they are proportionately more likely than whites to be arrested.

Laws Passed in Seattle Since 1985

New laws and ordinances implemented at the city and state level to reduce crime were powerful weapons for the police department's war on drugs and street criminals. Chambliss (1994) states that the war on drugs provided the police with a functional equivalent to riots in the inner city.

Reporter Duff Wilson of the *Seattle Times* (January 17, 1993:BI) stated that when the war on drugs first set out to attack gangs and crack cocaine, it was obvious that young African-American men would be the first and easiest targets.

> But from the Statehouse in Olympia to the precinct house on Seattle's South Myrtle Street, few knew it would go so far. Judges and other criminal justice experts are now saying the cumulative effect of drug laws passed over the past decade is patently unfair to Black men— punishing them more often and more harshly than anyone else.

As Seattle was implementing its token form of community policing, community policing advocates and Seattle police officials were pressing politicians in Olympia to implement tougher laws to deal with gangs and crack cocaine. For instance, a 1989 state law gave two extra years of prison time to anyone caught selling drugs within 1,000 feet of a school, but it appeared that the law was being vigorously enforced in only one part of King County, in the Seattle central district. According to Wilson, the first 24 people hit with this law were all African-American males. This is consistent with Chambliss' (1994) view that African-American males are a population without political clout or resources and with a public image in which crime is endemic.

A 1990 Seattle ordinance allowed police to arrest suspected drug dealers for loitering. With the aid of the SSCPC, the police department started a vigorous campaign to do something about crime to satisfy the diverse law-abiding communities in Seattle. In 1992, the department's Operation Hardfall, a well-publicized sting operation, resulted in drug trafficking charges against 88 people. Seventy-three people pleaded guilty or were found guilty at Operation Hardfall trials, charges were dropped against six, and just one person was acquitted.

One of the more controversial laws, Washington State's Community Protection Act, was passed July 1, 1990, and is commonly known as "The Predator Law." This law was passed to control the state's sexual offenders. Its provision for indefinite civil commitment for sexually violent predators became the focus of intense political, legal, and media debate (Websdale, 1994).

The enforcement of specific laws to reduce high-profile crimes demonstrates that the police department was influenced by external pressures. As an integral partner and team member of the entire criminal justice community, the police cannot stand alone from the prosecutor's office, the city jail, or the mayor's office. Also, the assistance of community organizations and downtown businesses is needed to appear legitimate before the city council and mayor. The police department relies on citizen lobbying to influence legislation to help them do its job, especially in high-crime areas and "hot spots." New laws resulted in sweeps and dragnets of the inner city population.

NET WIDENING AND SOCIAL CONTROL IN SEATTLE

The laws enforced by Seattle police illustrate net widening in action. The police organization was willing to grow and expand its organizational control mechanisms. It is important to note that state legislatures and powerful prosecutor associations aided and abetted police organizations in this ideological war on crime with laws and ordinances to arrest street-level offenders.

Events in Seattle corresponded with Brogden's (1982) research on the British police's implementation of community policing and the subsequent widening of social control. He notes that within the broad rubric of the community policing program, two general forms of police work can be distinguished. The first is race relations work, and the second is community involvement schemes (both of which have been discussed previously). Brogden contends that community policing represents the zenith of police intervention in civil society through the medium of legal relations. Furthermore, community policing has particular attraction for officials as an ideological premise, and the way that, as a creed, it satisfies the representative of social classes and of political lobbies. Tactically, it allows consent to be constructed at a political level (Brogden, 1982). The politicization of street crime unites law enforcement authorities and politicians together against crime.

The 15-Point Plan for South Seattle (Central District)

Community policing and the war on drugs allowed consent and legitimacy to be subtly constructed at the political level in Seattle. The 15-Point Plan (Appendix B) is illustrative of the SSCPC's attempt to gain legitimacy in the eyes of the Seattle Police Department.

The SSCPC fashioned the 15-Point Plan after long-term negotiations and presented it to the Seattle Police Department (Fleissner et al., 1991). Approximately 10 members of the SSCPC met with South Precinct commanders and the chief over a 10-month period. The plan widened the net of social control by the police department in conjunction with the SSCPC, a group with an assortment of names and hidden agendas (Scheingold, 1991). According to Fleissner et al. (1991), this was the first time in United States history that a police department entered into a contract with a community group. The primary purpose of this contract was to have the police department buy into the group's conception of the crime problem and crime targets.

The 15-Point Plan illustrated organizational decision-making and damage control. The chief appears to have entered into this relationship to placate the SSCPC and to gain this resource-rich group's assistance in setting targets for Seattle's version of community policing and the war on drugs. The SSCPC was attempting to co-opt the department into buying their conception of how the two sectors of the south end (the Robert sector and the Sam sector) should be patrolled and policed. The primary focus of this public relations policing effort was to influence the police department under the guise of "what the community wants."

The 15-Point Plan may have been written in such general terms that it had no real meaning. For example, the 13th point (if the department lacks sufficient funds for equipment, the community will have a fund-raising campaign) is automatic because a department never has sufficient funds to solve all of its crime problems or calls regarding disorder.

It seems that the police chief led this group into believing that he was going to let them nominate and control the crime agenda, when in reality, it may have been a public relations ploy. It was sophisticated in that it represented, as Brogden (1982) states, the height of police intervention in civil society. Street crime was a minor problem in the south end, but community policing was highly politicized by all of the actors involved.

Organizational Decision-Making and Damage Control

When the SSCPC presented the 15-Point Plan to the department, the police chief reconstructed the plan to suit the police department's needs. The adoption of this plan illustrated the department's decision-making process and how it attempted to control any damage to its image that may or may not occur from citizens' perception of the department not doing something about street crime. The department did not want the media to portray it as callous and unconcerned about marginalized citizens. This illustrates that internal proceeding shape any organization's relationship with the outside world (Bouza, 1990).

Co-opting Local Groups and Widening the Net

The police chief indicated that the SSCPC was one of the reasons that community policing was implemented in Seattle. Other officials interviewed agreed with the police chief's view. The center piece of the plan was to have SSCPC leaders and supporters help the police department set targets for crime control and prevention. Early in his term, the chief was involved in police-community committees, negotiating and co-opting local groups into helping police programs and activities. His career in New York City had prepared him for the process-oriented politics and the growth of street crime and disorder in Seattle.

Interview with SSCPC Leader

When the leader of the SSCPC was interviewed, he indicated that the philosophy of community policing meant police partnership-type activities and the police and community working together to clearly define targets and activities (personal interview, 1993). When questioned about why there should be community policing in Seattle, he responded, "because it works, and it has led to an eight percent crime decrease." When questioned about achievements of community policing in Seattle, he felt that it had created more sensitivity from the police. When asked about decentralization and community policing, he said that each precinct is different and the police department should work on management from within. When questioned about whether community policing reduced disorder in the South Seattle community, the SSCPC representative stated that it emphasized the positive. He gave credit to the 15-Point Plan for leading to a reduction in burglaries and improving the quality of life in the local community. He believed that community policing defined the problems, and then the problems subsided. When questioned about who defined the crime problems in Seattle, he said that the community defined problems and picked out targets. He said community policing addressed "any and everything." He reported that the teams issued over 600 citations for garbage in people's yards and old abandoned cars. He noted that the compliance was around 95 percent. He went on to say that the community policing teams "solve an amazing number of problems. They provide follow-up and closure for crime-related problems." When questioned about what led to community policing teams in Seattle, he indicated that it was "consciousness on the part of the community and that community people had to go through institutional structures." When questioned whether police training had changed with the advent of community policing, he indicated "sensitivity training/diversity."

One of the purposes of implementing community policing in Seattle was to improve police-community relationships in pockets of the community where relationships were poor and perceptions of the Seattle Police Department were low. The SSCPC leader was well-educated, influential, and articulate, and organized the property owners in the south end. The police department was willing to work with this individual and the SSCPC because they were amenable to the department's vision of community policing. The SSCPC did not want to change the police department's internal structure or upset the status quo. They wanted to decrease persistent street crime and disorder in the south end. Most important, the 15-Point Plan was utilized by the SSCPC to gain both short-term and long-term commitments from the police department regarding street-level crime and disorder in their district and local neighborhoods.

SEATTLE POLICE DEPARTMENT AND THE MICRO-MANAGEMENT OF THE WEED & SEED CONTROVERSY (1992-1993)

What we know about the Seattle Police Department and the internal decision-making process and conflicts regarding the implementation of the federal Weed & Seed program in early 1992 comes from news articles, city council hearing transcripts (which involved the police chief), federal documents, the police department proposal, and interviews conducted in Seattle with police officials and community residents. The stated purpose of the Weed & Seed program was to "pull out the weeds that choke off opportunity and begin to sow the seeds of community revitalization. The essence of Weed & Seed is the coordinated effort between crime-fighting forces and community development forces" (Operation Weed and Seed Implementation Manual, 1992:2).

Community policing and Weed & Seed were linked together programmatically and must be conceptually viewed as both organizational growth and programmatic add-ons. Public officials in Seattle followed the guidelines of linking the program to community policing, which made Weed & Seed easier to implement and maintain. The Operation Weed and Seed Implementation Manual (1992) stated that community policing was a bridge between Weed & Seed. It also stated that community policing would increase police visibility and develop cooperative relationships between police and citizens in target areas. This strategy would provide a bridge to prevention, intervention, and treatment, and to neighborhood reclamation and restoration. Officers on foot patrol meeting the residents, citizen neighborhood watches, and community relations activities would increase positive interaction between police and neighborhood residents and help reduce drug use, trafficking, and related crime. The manual visualizes a holistic approach to crime control, reduction, and prevention. Theoretically, the program manual suggests a law enforcement consortium and an assortment of actors eagerly involved in the war on crime and criminals. It further visualizes a 1990s poverty program with punching power and supportive linkages.

Weed & Seed affected the Seattle Police Department internally because the planning section of the inspectional services division wrote the grant proposal. The city council held public hearings that were contentious and reflective of years of conflict between the local community and the police department. The mayor's office and the city council were placed in a reactive position to defend the proposal and the selection of the central district as the target area for the implementation of the federal program. The mayor attempted to persuade federal government officials to change the name of the program. The final proposal was not accepted for over nine months.

It is important to note that community policing teams were not formally instituted in the four precincts of the Seattle Police Department until January 1990. Weed & Seed was an add-on and bridge for the police department to implement community policing in Seattle's central district. The research revealed that no discussion of implementing the Weed & Seed program in the south end or citywide ever took place. The controversy arose because the mayor proposed to place the Weed & Seed program in the central district *only*, and the residents of that district fought against its implementation *only* in their neighborhoods.

Politics of Community Policing and Weed & Seed (External Pressures)

Gil Habadayshi (Department of Justice Community Relations Office in Seattle) stated that the emotions regarding the Weed & Seed program ran high (personal interview, 1993). First, the Seattle Police Department planning unit wrote the application for the grant. Second, damage was done by the planning process, which included only government actors and excluded the general public and the residents of the target area—the central district. He noted that the mayor's office suggested the central district for the implementation of the Weed & Seed program. Also, he said that in some cities, the whole community shared the Weed & Seed funds, including Atlanta, Denver, and Cleveland. He confirmed that the merger of Weed & Seed with community policing was a false marriage. He noted that in the whole department, only six officers per precinct were involved with the community policing teams. Most important, he mentioned that race, crime, and perceptions of the police were conspicuous in Seattle around the Weed & Seed controversy (personal interview, 1993).

Media Impact

To understand the politics of linking the two programs, one must appreciate the power and impact of the local media (i.e., newspaper editorials), and its relationship to the Seattle Police Department. Williamson's *Seattle Times* article on April 19, 1992:A10, states that the concept of Weed & Seed sounds good, "but it seems to depend on who's doing the listening." The article continues:

> Seattle Police say it is a way to get money—$1.1 million this year, with a potential of $10 million over the next four years—for a financially strapped police department and bolster the community policing concept. Many residents in Seattle's Central Area—home of "the targeted neighborhood"—say it is the imposition of open season on young African-American males and a way to violate the civil liberties of an entire community.

Williamson declared that these two perceptions were "pretty far apart."

Williamson attended a Stop the Violence community meeting held in the central district at Garfield High School to try to find a middle ground between the two diverse perspectives. He discovered that there were community problems, and the Weed & Seed program was only a minor issue on the agenda. Concerned citizens attending the meeting were angry, frustrated, and frightened about recent events in the community and were in no mood for a workshop on Weed & Seed. A week earlier, six people had been killed and three seriously wounded in a "bloody, insane weekend in the Seattle area," reported Williamson. The citizens wanted to discuss problems in the community such as schools, affordable housing, jobs, community leadership, health care, and other real life issues they felt were not being addressed in the central district. The author attended a similar rally at the high school after a drive-by shooting. The chief and the deputy mayor of public safety were in attendance. This is a reflection of the ongoing disorganization and frustration in the central district of Seattle (Taylor, 1994).

On December 3, 1992, the Seattle City Council Public Safety Committee held a public hearing on revising the Weed & Seed application. The police chief attended the public hearing and discussed the importance of using community policing officers to implement the Weed & Seed program and fight crime in the central district. Eighty-seven people attended the hearing. Thirty-nine people signed in as for Weed & Seed, and 48 against. Margaret Pageler, chair of the committee, introduced the city council members and informed the public that the meeting was a hearing on the revision of the Weed &

Seed application. The mayor and police chief understood the power and impact a citizens' group could have on the internal workings of their respective offices and departments. Therefore, they needed to listen to the comments of both the pro and con sides of the issue. Listening is very important in Seattle and other cities that practice process-oriented government. The ultimate goal is to arrive at consensus and understanding. To help understand the controversy and heated discussion regarding the implementation of the Weed & Seed program in the central district only, one needs to appreciate both sides of the issue and its subtle impact on Seattle Police Department management.

Citizen Views Supporting Weed & Seed

Most of the individuals who were pro-Weed & Seed were also supportive of the department's version of community policing in the central district, and of policing in general. At the public hearing held by the Seattle City Council Public Safety Committee, several activists and concerned citizens offered their support for the police department, the city council, and the small community policing teams. Several of their comments and statements are outlined below.

George Stuart, a central district community leader, urged the council to pass the Weed & Seed proposal. He said that Weed & Seed emphasis is on community policing programs. He also noted that historically, the relationship between the police and the community has been poor (personal interview, 1993).

Faye Christian urged the passage of Weed & Seed so that the central district would know that "we haven't been surrendered to drugs and gangs" (personal interview, 1993).

Mark Stepper indicated that the "paranoia" about Weed & Seed is unfounded. "We need tougher laws, especially regarding firearms. We need increased police surveillance. We need more social programs. We can't afford to turn this money down with cuts in state funding" (personal interview, 1993).

Robert Perry declared that not only black youths are being targeted. "It bothers me that we are making assumptions about our police force without knowing them" (personal interview, 1993).

Harilyn Bobis said, "I first moved to the central area because it is integrated. Now there are gangs, guns, and violence. I charge the city council to protect me" (personal interview, 1993).

Chris Acala related, "We can't walk in our community, play in front yards. We are being solicited for drugs, sex, and experience drive-by shootings. The community is willing to forge a working relationship with the police" (personal interview, 1993).

Ken Hunt stated, "We need help. We're trying to combat the drug problem ourselves. We don't think we should have to do this alone" (personal interview, 1993).

Margaret Ellis indicated, "Our civil rights have been taken away by gangs and drugs. We need help and want it. We need social programs and jobs too but need to get rid of these drug dealers who don't live in our neighborhood" (personal interview, 1993).

Louise Loflin said, "Our community spends time arguing over Weed & Seed and another child goes to drugs. We must attack the drug problem on every level. There are many solutions to the problem and Weed & Seed is one of them" (personal interview, 1993).

David Myles stated, "I worry about the neighborhood. I wish everyone testifying here would read the Weed & Seed proposal" (personal interview, 1993).

Based on this author's research, this was a close-knit group that was multi-racial, socially locked in low-income pockets of the central district, and very frustrated with street criminals.

Views of Citizens Opposed to Weed & Seed

At the same public hearing, several residents voiced their opposition to the implementation of the Weed & Seed program in the central district. Generally speaking, many of the individuals had been fighting police department policies for years. Their responses are summarized below.

Squakee said that she did not agree with Weed & Seed. "The seed money doesn't come to people that need it. Parents need the money and the jobs" (personal interview, 1993).

Don Alexander indicated, "This proposal is just lies and playing with words. We're doing the same thing again. We will give you Weed & Seed with more administrators and more police" (personal interview, 1993).

L.S. declared, "More police will exacerbate the problem. We are 'reseeded' out. We need economic development and banks that other neighborhoods have" (personal interview, 1993).

Fred Hyde said, "The solution is not to lock up young black men but to get jobs. [New] Weed & Seed is no different than the old Weed & Seed" (personal interview, 1993).

Zackary Rivera stated, "We shouldn't be trying to put more cops on the street. We know you are going to pass Weed & Seed. This will make people more angry and frustrated and we will revolt" (personal interview, 1993).

Muffy Sunda declared, "Weed & Seed will be police against the community. Mayor Rice never came back to the community like he promised, but he came back with a revised Weed & Seed" (personal interview, 1993).

Raymond Miller said, "Weed & Seed concentrates on anti-drug activities in the inner city and further exacerbates the tension between police and the African-American community. There is a danger of ties with Weed & Seed and assistance for inner cities to the United States Attorney and local police oversights. Weed & Seed has generated broad-based community opposition, and the program will fail to receive community support and thus will fail" (personal interview, 1993).

Gordon McHenry stated, "Weed & Seed addresses some issues. If Weed & Seed is adopted, we need strong citizen presence and have it administered by civilians" (personal interview, 1993).

Harriet Walden indicated, "It is a racist program. The implementation creates a two tier system. The mayor promised he would come back to our community, and he hasn't. We need a police review board with subpoena power" (personal interview, 1993).

Lonnie Nelson declared, "The Weed & Seed program pushes the problems into other neighborhoods" (personal interview, 1993).

Omar Salisbury (personal interview, 1993) stated:

Everybody here is old. I'm in high school. You need to get out and help the neighborhood. Not every person in a gang is bad or evil. They are looking for a family, for someone who cares about them. When was the last time you talked to people or walked the street. You don't get harassed by the police like we do. Come out to the central area— come out to Garfield High.

On the one hand, those in favor of Weed & Seed supported some form of crime control and prevention activities by the Seattle Police Department in the central district, and argued that the Weed & Seed monies should not be turned down. On the other hand, the comments of those opposed were characterized by skepticism toward the police and demands for greater police accountability on the streets of the central district rather than more federal monies. Under close scrutiny, these two opposing groups' values and public articulation were not that different. Both wanted an end to street-level drug dealing, gangs, gang violence, and community apathy. However, the pro group was willing to accept heavy-handed police tactics to rid the streets of the central district of criminals, gangs, and riffraff. The con group was reluctant to accept the police law-and-order tactics to fight street-level criminals, gangs, and riffraff. Many of the con group leaders became involved in crime prevention because their sons and daughters had been intimidated by the police.

The Seattle City Council voted six to three in support of Weed & Seed. The mayor won a hard and bitter nine-month battle over a program he wanted to implement in the central district. The police department received the federal funds to do the weeding and won the hard-fought battle to gain legitimacy for the chief and the department in the central district. The new monies allowed the police department to hire a few officers in the East Precinct to implement the Weed & Seed program in the central district. This process has previously been described as organizational add-ons.

INTERNAL PRESSURES

The Seattle Police Department tried to maneuver through internal pressures to create what has come to be defined as a model for community policing. Internally, the department hired auditors and consultants to improve the police image in the public's eye, utilized proactive deployment strategies, tried to placate community policing team officers, and used internal affairs and investigations to control press releases and publicity. Middle level management made no commitment to implementing true community policing department-wide because there was no real commitment in the upper management. Only small specialty units were placed in each precinct and called community policing teams. The community policing advocates wanted more of the community policing teams throughout the entire city.

Auditors and Consultants

Former municipal judge Terrence Carroll was appointed by the mayor in 1991 to study the system of investigating complaints against Seattle police officers. He ultimately recommended no civilian review board to oversee police discipline. This researcher discovered that when the city faced an issue or problem that was potentially embarrassing, they hired someone close to and/or supportive of the administration to diffuse or offer a solution to the problem.

In 1989, Carroll Buracher and Associates recommended that the department look closely at its operation and expand the small community policing teams to all four precincts. In this report, the authors suggested that the department needed to increase the number of police officers in the department. Of the two auditors and consultants listed above, most of the fervor came from the findings of the Terrence Carroll audit, which recommended no civilian review board. The American Civil Liberties Union (ACLU) of Washington state, the city council, the mayor's office, and local community leaders became involved in the debate over whether or not to have a review board. The ACLU wanted a review board, while the city council and mayor's office wanted to consider it further. Some community leaders wanted the review board as a means of controlling police misconduct, and some community leaders were not involved with the issue.

The auditors and consultants were brought in by city leaders to politically massage the various interests in the city's political game around the issues of a civilian review board, control of the police, and the new community policing movement.

Community Policing Advocates and Proactive Deployment Strategies

There was enormous internal pressure by a small cadre of officers in the Seattle Police Department to develop some kind of alternative to the reactive 911 system and establish lasting relationships with local community groups. The officers the researcher spoke with felt that the methods and tactics being utilized to combat crime were not working and constantly argued that there would never be enough resources (e.g., funds and manpower) to respond adequately to crime in the traditional manner. In 1990, James C. Scott (Executive Director of the Washington State Criminal Justice Training Commission) wrote a position paper on community policing, in which he stated that community policing focuses on prevention of crime, and is the only strategy that has proven successful in the era of static and dwindling resources. Furthermore, Scott noted that community policing was probably the most effective way of fighting drug abuse and gang violence. In several interviews conducted with officers at the rank of lieutenant and sergeant, the researcher found that some officers wanted to get involved in a comprehensive yet proactive deployment strategy that permeated the entire department.

Several local political leaders were feeling the pressure from Washington, D.C. to do more with less. At the heart of community policing is do more with less on the one hand, and the reality of implementing a full-blown version of true community policing on the other. Community policing is labor intensive and depends heavily on community involvement and linkages. Scheingold (1991) made the statement that, in effect, community policing joins the community to help police managers avoid the kinds of excessive force that create serious political problems.

Internal Affairs and Investigations

There were enormous pressures internally (within the Seattle Police Department and within city agencies) to clean up the department's internal affairs operations, including the investigation of officers. For instance, during the summer of 1993, the Seattle Human Rights Commission director indicated that his office had received numerous complaints about individual officers' behavior since the late 1980s and early 1990s. The complainants did not have trust in the police department's internal affairs and investigation unit, according to the director. Consequently, they complained to the Human Rights Commission, which they felt more comfortable talking with because there were racial minorities on the staff.

A copy of a 1990 Human Rights Commission report recommended that the police department create a civilian team of two to work side by side with internal investigation systems as they investigate cases. The civilian team would report to the Human Rights Commission and make independent recommendations to the Chief of Police. The Human Rights Commission was getting so many complaints regarding police abuse that the director, Bill Hilliard, met with the chief on several occasions regarding the allegations during the late 1980s (Reed, 1995).

The mayor formally received complaints about police misconduct in early 1990. He issued an executive order to the Seattle Police Department to end incidents of brutality. The mayor's order made the Seattle Police Department appear negligent to the other city departments and the general public. The chief sought to regain internal legitimacy and credibility with his officers and other city officials. After the mayor's executive order, the chief attended roll call in each of the four precincts and urged his officers to be cautious and pay particular attention to their handling of each case on the streets. Consequently, this led to decreases of allegations of police brutality, according to Hilliard. In a February 10, 1992 memo, Hilliard applauded the police chief for the wonderful success and the decrease of charges filed with his department under the mayor's executive order, which alleged police misconduct. "You and your department are to be commended for a twenty-month decrease in reports and allegations of police misconduct," stated Hilliard (personal interview, February 10, 1992).

One of the attractions of a token form of community policing is to gain symbolic linkages with community activists and to assert that the mayor, police department, and city council are doing something about crime and are concerned about officer behavior on the streets.

The department faced intense external pressure to develop and implement an internal civilian review board. Several vocal groups in the central district fought unsuccessfully for years for such a board. The mayor and police chief responded by appointing former judge Terrence Carroll to deal internally with allegations of police abuse of citizens. The ex-judge failed to support any changes in responding to allegations of police brutality and helped maintain the status quo regarding civilian review. He indicated that a few bad apples did exist in the Seattle Police Department, but, by and large, the majority of the officers did an outstanding job (Carroll, 1993).

The former judge's internal investigation report indicated that there were police officers who used poor judgment and made mistakes and should receive training and corrective action. He noted that, in general, the public believes that a fair system is in place to discipline and, if appropriate, to assist officers who step out of line. The former judge was an integral part of the urban political process and served as a buffer to legitimate the police department to the general public.

The buffers helped the department to maintain legitimacy in the eyes of some individuals who complained about officer behavior, and it helped maintain the balance of government, particularly relationships between the mayor, police chief, and city council.

Middle-Level Management

Scheingold (1991) makes the statement that police managers, rather than rank-and-file officers, have been more resistant to community policing because they are uneasy about relinquishing organizational control. He also purports that community policing gives police managers a way to minimize politically explosive confrontations between the police and the public, especially in black and minority communities.

Kelling and Bratton (1993) report that three sources of resistance seem to be paramount in the minds of police executives as they look at implementing community policing. The first source of resistance is unions, the second is detectives, and the third is middle-level management.

Unions

In the Seattle Police Department, the union was the strongest of the sources of resistance outlined by Kelling and Bratton. Seattle had two unions, one for street-level officers and the other for upper management. These unions resisted any changes that would jeopardize the traditional bureaucratic organizational structure, including civilian review boards. Union members supported the position of auditor ex-judge Terrence Carroll, particularly the street-level officers' union represented by Sergeant Ed Striedinger, who is on record as supporting Carroll's findings.

Detectives

Throughout the new community policing craze, community policing advocates have lost sight of detectives and their strong commitment to investigative follow-up. Consequently, detectives are not that interested in the new policing philosophy as espoused by Trojanowicz (1990), Goldstein (1990), and others, primarily because it means they would lose their influence over some cases. The jargon of community policing alleges that the community policing officer will be a mini-chief within his assigned area. If this is in fact true, many detectives will not buy into the philosophy of community policing.

Community policing advocates in Seattle paid almost no attention to the role of detective work. Therefore, entrenched detectives are against community policing teams, community policing, and any new innovations. The detective's role is being diminished and usurped by the street police. The police on the street have more power than before and wider authoritative latitude to do their job. Therefore, the detectives feel like they are in a lesser role because the street police are more prestigious and influential than before the advent of community policing.

Mid-Management

Kelling and Bratton (1993) report that community policing experiences in other cities suggest that when middle-level managers are involved in the process of planning innovations, they are capable of providing instrumental leadership. However, this research found no evidence of middle-level management resistance or support to the token form of community policing in Seattle. In fact, based on interviews conducted, it is this author's opinion that many were not even asked for their input on implementing community policing. Community policing, as it was implemented in Seattle, seemed to be no threat to anyone in the department.

CHAPTER SUMMARY

Blue uniform policing between 1985 and 1993 in Seattle can be characterized as having a range of functions, namely, enforcing (and sometimes defining) the criminal law, maintaining order, and securing consent, all directed toward a singular end: upholding the general legal framework of the state. Scheingold (1991) states that community policing might turn punitive, and seems destined to extend significantly the reach of the state. Brogden et al. (1988) note that police work is about securing and maintaining consent or ideological control in order to facilitate the reproduction of order in society. It appears that the Seattle Police Department was subtly involved in maintaining consent, ideological control, and legitimation. Most important, it helped define the criminal law and maintain order. Thus, the term "blue uniform" policing accurately describes activities in Seattle in the period 1985-1993.

It has been illustrated that community policing had a diversity of meanings in Seattle, and many neighborhood leaders interviewed offered tacit support for the police department's version of community policing. However, most of the residents in the central district wanted more community policing teams and humane policing to help solve community and street-level problems. Several individuals told the researcher that they felt over-policed and under-protected.

In addition, the implementation of several new laws widened the net of social control in Seattle as the department experimented with community policing. Community policing and Weed & Seed led to the widening of informal social control procedures on the streets of Seattle. The Seattle city government (mayor's office, city council, and Seattle Police Department) worked together subtly to construct consent and maintain legitimacy. One of the key ideas behind winning consent from the governed is to hide deep-seated social pressures, conflicts, and contradictions from donors and big business executives. Winning consent also tells us that there is a chance for change for organized groups. The pressures around Weed & Seed indicated that such is the case. However, the government controls the winning and manufacturing of consent. Police organizations face multiple internal, political, and economic pressures to change. Harring (1983) argues that the police function's overall goal has remained the same since its conception. Police departments are placed in a reactive mode when called upon to manage and control crises and external political pressures not of their making. Police are the cornerstone or the control mechanism and the legitimation process. Police officers police the underclass and those needing law enforcement services the most.

However, Kappeler and Kraska (1997) report that police today use corporate metaphors, community rhetoric, and the expansion of scientifically deployed social control. These changes are making the police institution even more valuable in the sociotechnics of a changing society. These authors further report that policing seized the metaphors of market economics and rhetoric of community in an age where some have questioned the extent to which either of these traditional social forms still exists.

As for the Seattle police organization, Kennedy (1993) reports that there are four widely held beliefs about policing society. First, the public demand for police services, particularly 911 rapid-response services, is out of police control. Second, department resources are already deployed efficiently and effectively. Third, community policing is a discretionary add-on to the core job of policing because it is seen as "soft." Fourth, police resources (police department budgets) are largely static, particularly in the current climate of fiscal restraint. Kennedy suggests that if the chief supports these beliefs, the largest gains a department can hope to make are small improvements in patrol deployment. He is not surprised that police organizations find large increases in calls for services, or striking new challenges like the crack epidemic and waves of youth violence, very difficult to meet. Kennedy's research indicates that none of these four beliefs are true. However, many departments maintain the status quo after research, audits, and close scrutiny regarding standard operating procedures.

The Seattle Police Department as an organization is best reflective of belief number three as outlined above. This research showed that community policing was constructed to be a discretionary add-on to the core job of traditional policing. Community policing was viewed by top administrative officials as soft on crime. Micro-organizational processes and related theory helped analyze the organizational characteristics and dynamics that framed the development of community policing in Seattle in the period 1985-1993.

CHAPTER 6

Community Policing in Seattle: A "Model" Partnership Between Citizens and Police

This chapter analyzes and summarizes the influences that led the Seattle Police Department to develop and implement a model for community policing in Seattle, Washington, between 1985 and 1993.

OVERVIEW: THE CASE OF COMMUNITY POLICING IN SEATTLE

This research examined the development of community policing in Seattle, Washington (1985-1993). Significant internal and external political pressures led the Seattle Police Department to adopt a modified version of community policing. Community policing, an increasingly influential approach to law enforcement, has been defined by its proponents as a model partnership between citizens and police (Fleissner et al., 1992). In theory, the basic characteristics of community policing are personalized policing, where the same officer patrols the same area on a permanent basis; the use of a decentralized mini-station or storefront; and collaboration with citizens to identify and solve crime problems (Greene and Mastrofski, 1988; McElroy, Cosgrove, and Sadd, 1993; Trojanowicz and Bucqueroux, 1994; Rosenbaum, 1994). Police are no longer crime fighters; they become actively engaged in reordering social space, organizing social relations, and regulating disorder (Kappeler and Kraska, 1997). Widespread support exists in many quarters for police department decentralization, permanent assignments, and the development of citizen-police partnerships with local communities (Goldstein, 1990, 1993).

In theory, recent innovations such as community-oriented policing and problem-solving policing involve a radical reformation of what police do and have done traditionally. Because full adoption of both philosophies would involve substantial changes, including the leveling of the bureaucratic hierarchy, one can expect resistance to such innovations from within a police department and the local community (Carter and Radelet, 1994). As a matter of fact, recent community policing articles claim that pressures come internally from police unions, middle management, and rank-and-file officers. External pressures come from community-based organizations, residents who are fed up with crime, and individuals seeking to influence the police department. Trojanowicz (1993) suggests that pressures for community policing come from citizens' groups. On the other hand, Brown (1993) indicates that pressures for community policing come from leadership within the police organization. Both agree that internal and external pressures and recent police research explain the experimentation with and implementation of community policing in the 1980s and 1990s (Reed, 1995).

The contemporary popularity of community policing in Seattle was stimulated by the apparent failure of traditional police-control strategies to slow the rate of growth of street crime and public disorder. The tension in Seattle brought on by change was further heightened by strong public demands that police do something about the street-crime problem and public disorders. Many middle- and upper-class commuters expected to travel unmolested through low-income/high-crime areas to get downtown. And, at times, different sectors of the public seemed to prefer different police practices for controlling street crime.

The central district and south end communities argued about police practices and crime-prevention strategies. Residents in the central district perceived that tough talking by politicians about law and order meant controlling people of color rather than controlling or preventing crime. Generally, residents in the south end were concerned about street crime and were led by a group of neighborhood political activists who were concerned about controlling criminals and crime. Thus, in addressing the crime problem, the Seattle Police Department often found itself negotiating between pressures emanating from the public and from its own internal politics between 1985 and 1993.

Despite internal and external struggles, the police department in Seattle, Washington, seems to have maneuvered through political pressures to create what has come to be defined as a model for community policing. Community policing in Seattle was a way of policing social and economic class divisions so as to avoid the serious public conflicts that have plagued policing in recent years (Brogden et al., 1988). In this book, particular attention was paid to the way in which the actual practice of community policing in Seattle was the result of the interaction between the community and police department politics rather than the simple bureaucratic implementation of a rational strategy of crime control. Long-term negotiation and compromise between the police and the community went into what is defined as a model citizen-police partnership. Community policing in Seattle could best be described as organizational add-ons, police public relations activities, co-optation of local conflict, and, finally, compromise and negotiation with the South Seattle Crime Prevention Council.

MAJOR THEORETICAL CONTRIBUTIONS

Three theoretical approaches contribute to this exploratory study of a social institution: legitimation processes, urban political processes, and micro-organizational processes. This is a unique qualitative case study of the politics of a national policy (community policing) as it was implemented at the local level.

Community policing sells itself as a new approach that involves working with the public to reduce street crime, fear of street crime, and public disorder. "Community" is a public sphere concept, and does not include certain forms of private behaviors that are criminal, socially harmful, and widespread. Among these forms of socially harmful behaviors are domestic violence and corporate crime. Community policing is unable to control these behaviors because they happen behind closed doors.

When community policing is scrutinized as a public sphere activity, its distinctiveness from other, more traditional, forms of policing begins to disappear. Rather, community policing, like other forms of policing, appears to reproduce the status quo with regards to various sets of historically enduring power relations; that is, those of class, gender, and race.

The legitimacy of community policing lies in its ability to present itself in terms of the language of caring and building consensus.

However, when critically scrutinized, community policing may be just one more way of keeping women subordinate in homes, corporate executives out of jail, and racial minorities in their place.

Robinson et al. (1994:149) raise an important question about the possibility of community policing in a society that by definition must produce a police in its own image. They conclude that the possibility of producing an egalitarian police from an inegalitarian society is about the same as "expecting a swan to emerge from a hen's egg."

Legitimation processes suggest that broader fiscal issues of the state are at work whenever scholars study postmodern cities such as Seattle. An examination of urban political processes reveals how city government addresses social and political issues such as the growth in crime, homelessness, and unemployment. Micro-organizational processes that focus on planned changes help us appreciate how traditional police bureaucratic organizations resist change and attempt to adapt, and, in some cases, negotiate, compromise, or co-opt issues of crime control and prevention with neighborhood and community-based organizations.

As we have seen, multiple political and economic forces shape policing strategies. The Seattle Police Department was forced to play a reactive role in order to manage and control external pressures. Much of policing is reactive, as many departments are not good at proactive-type policing activities (Williams and Wagoner, 1995). Consequently, the Seattle Police Department developed a subtle proactive plan to maintain the department's legitimation in the eyes of the various publics. Small community policing teams were set up as a proactive mechanism to respond to pressures from the two communities.

Community policing serves powerful organized political interests. It was a political and public relations success in Seattle. The police department and city hall wanted to be perceived as doing something positive about menacing street crime and public disorders. Community policing both in Seattle and nationwide helps us understand the proactive nature of policing in the 1990s. When police respond proactively, it is usually due to internal pressure from top administration, which is often in turn a response to an external pressure on the department to do something about street crime (Williams and Wagoner, 1995).

An understanding of urban political processes and legitimation processes also helps us make sense of *external* pressures on the Seattle Police Department. Finally, the *internal* pressures on the police to do something about street crime and public disorder are typical of the functions of micro-organizational processes. Within social organizations there are bureaucratic rules that have to be followed, and organizations typically resist change and the loss of resources. The Seattle Police Department managed both internal and external political pressures to benefit the legitimacy of its organization and the urban government officials and politicos.

POLITICS OF COMMUNITY POLICING REVISITED

According to Manning (1995), the American police are, in theory, apolitical. However, in practice, the police organization functions in a political context. The purpose of community policing in Seattle was to do something about street crime in neighborhoods with a high volume of gun violence, and to reduce the number of crimes that contributed to physical and social disorder and neighborhood decay (Seattle Police Department 1991-1995 Long Range Plan, 1992). However, the Seattle Police Department made no commitment to community policing beyond a demonstration project utilizing 30 officers out of a uniformed force of over 1,200 (Bereano, 1993). In other words, there was one community policing officer for every 16,666 residents in the city—at best a limited partnership in the overall context of Seattle policing.

The Seattle Police Department instituted community police teams citywide in 1990, and the focus of training was on effective public speaking, not the philosophy of community policing as advocated by Goldstein, Trojanowicz, and other law enforcement scholars. The point being made here is that time was spent on matters which did not directly pertain to protecting and serving citizens. Thus, community policing teams were basically police public relations teams with good public speaking skills. Furthermore, the community policing teams were examples of top-down policing, where policies and procedures for crime control and prevention emanate from the chief down to the lowest level of the community. The Seattle Police Department was the "expert" for the local community, and residents were implored to accept the police version of activities that would help them solve their street crime problems.

To some, community policing teams were simply crime control programs incorporated into the precincts to improve the tenuous relationship between inner city residents and the Seattle Police Department. Historically, Seattle's African-American and minority communities had a long history of conflict and strained relations with the police department.

Community policing and community policing teams were very political and reflected traditional policing with a new friendly face. The department seemed to engage in traditional policing with organizational add-ons. At first blush, these add-ons looked and sounded like prevention programs, but, in actuality, they were heavy-handed control activities. For instance, the Seattle Police Department reported in 1993 that emphasis patrols were used to concentrate police presence in hot spots identified by residents in the central district and the south end. Also, the same report noted that community policing teams supported and encouraged neighborhood anti-crime efforts, such as Stop the Violence vigils (Fleissner, et al., 1991, 1992).

Community policing in Seattle was more traditional policing than the model as articulated by national proponents such as Carter and Radelet (1994), Goldstein (1993), and Trojanowicz and Bucqueroux (1994). Trojanowicz and Bucqueroux (1994:3) define community policing as "a philosophy of full service personalized policing, where the same officer patrols and works in the same area on a permanent basis, from a decentralized place, working in partnership with citizens to identify and solve problems." The traditional policing organization remains intact, with new programs periodically added but no fundamental organizational changes occurring. It may be argued that the Seattle Police Department married community policing teams and traditional policing activities for expediency's sake, public relations ploys, and political gains.

In Seattle, community policing was not a rational crime-prevention or crime control model, but the result of political interaction among the community, police department, and local government. All of these actors were involved in the production and construction of programs to maintain the image of Seattle as a liveable and safe community for residents and new businesses. Most important, community policing in Seattle was the result of police department politics and the placating of an opportunistic and elitist community group. Community policing in Seattle was very ideological and crime control-oriented.

Legitimation processes were examined in light of whether or not they played a role in the development of community policing in Seattle. The author's expectation was that government requires a degree of consent, and police officers and officials must be seen as taking care of business on the streets. The community policing teams that were developed were found to be crime control programs and organizational add-ons. These community policing teams were programmatic in nature and heavy on public relations activities. Specifically, no structural changes in the department hierarchy were evidenced during the 1985-1993 period, nor was there an evaluation mechanism set up for the public to understand the purpose of community policing. The department was subtly involved in the development of, cohesion in, and regulation of the social system in the central district and south end neighborhoods. Legitimation processes played a role in the department, producing several crime-prevention and crime control programs in the two communities. These programs helped the department to maintain legitimacy in the eyes of the two communities' residents. The evidence gathered showed that the department and government officials wanted to be perceived as doing something about street crime rather than being passive or soft on crime.

The ways in which urban political processes affected the development of community policing in Seattle were examined. This author's expectation was that small businesses would have their needs met more so than unorganized and powerless groups. In several instances, the Seattle Police Department, the city council, and the mayor's office were subtly involved in implementing a form of community policing that would be acceptable to various publics and constituencies. All of the political actors were concerned about how Seattle was perceived by the residents and potential new businesses. They all wanted to be viewed as doing something about the urban landscape and downtown development, not as soft on crime or non-supportive of the aspirations of their constituents.

At first blush, community policing sounds revolutionary if one accepts its rhetoric. However, it is reformist in nature and seeks to maintain the status quo in a capitalist society (Reed, 1995). This is because reformist policies do not benefit the more marginal social groups, and most of the resources gained are highly symbolic and/or of an illusionary nature. The struggle around Weed & Seed in Seattle showed that citizen input and feedback does not guarantee a solution beneficial to both sides. Because community policing seeks to reproduce an ideal community in postmodern capitalist society, it is not about radical change, but passive revolution.

SEATTLE'S COMMUNITY POLICING EXPERIENCE

Seattle's experimentation with community policing in the 1990s succeeded in showing that influential middle-class citizens can shape the policy-making process of crime-prevention programs in inner city neighborhoods. It demonstrated that one police department can do something symbolic with crime-prevention and crime control programs.

The program did not achieve as much as expected. The program that was developed in Seattle involved community policing teams, neighborhood boards, and crime-prevention councils. It failed to measure up to the true spirit of community policing because it was only a token form of community policing instituted to soothe the reactionary neighborhood coalitions.

Would alternative strategies have led to a more successful or effective approach to community policing? The Seattle Police Department, in conjunction with the local community, could have spent more time developing a model precinct that focused on crime-prevention and crime control activities rather than instituting the Weed & Seed program in one community and passing it off as the panacea to the central district's problems. This model of citizen-police collaboration could have been adopted throughout the city.

Community policing has the potential to address street-level crime effectively. From a legitimation processes perspective, if fully formed, community policing teams would live in the area and become involved in daily life there. The potential exists for the neighborhood to accept the police, who would then be able to do something about street crime. From an urban political processes perspective, there is the potential for all of the major political actors to forge an alliance with communities and neighbors block-by-block to deal with street crime. However, a grand scheme or cure-all is destined to fail if not properly discussed, planned, and implemented. For example, Chicago invested resources in a five-year planning process to design and implement a community policing program (Rodriguez, 1997). From a micro-organizational processes perspective, a police department committed to mini-stations, storefronts, and community policing teams might make a difference in the lives of some apartment dwellers and public housing residents by realizing that citizens seeking police services want follow-up on particular crimes and incidents in their neighborhood. Also, some citizens would like legal ways to become involved and cooperate with the police in crime control and prevention efforts.

It is argued that community policing programs cannot be more than reformist programs within the capitalist political structure. Given the play of external interests, community policing cannot be expected to be more than a response to well-organized and affluent interests. Resource-rich community groups will always be able to "buy" the politicians and actors who set the agenda for public safety in a process-oriented government. In contrast, community groups that do not have resources or clout are at the mercy of city hall and powerful political actors.

Given the dynamics of police organizations, community policing has the potential to become more than a public relations effort that bolsters the image of police departments. Currently, the paramilitary structure of police departments impedes creative and innovative programs. Under the present political structure, there is a chance for community groups to police small pockets of neighborhoods and communities. However, if the community groups seek legitimacy, they must work within the organizational structure of the police department. In that respect, community policing is more than just a public relations exercise by the police department. Yet given current power relationships, it is impossible to visualize a form of community policing that does not enhance and bolster the public image of police departments. Police departments are an integral part of local government and law enforcement. Consequently, they are placed in a unique position to shape the public's consciousness about street crime in urban America.

FUTURE DIRECTIONS FOR COMMUNITY POLICING

Several proposals for the future of community policing have been offered. Bayley's (1994) blueprint theorizes that police do not and cannot prevent crime. He states that in order to prevent crime, modern police organizations must reorganize so that thinking takes priority over simply reacting to a situation. He alleges that the conventional police organization is preoccupied with the delivery of a small set of pre-packaged services—patrolling, responding rapidly, and criminal investigation. Furthermore, he indicates that police forces are dominated by line functions. Senior officers command, middle ranks supervise, and lower ranks execute. As a result, once delivery decisions are made by force commanders, the intricately rank-stratified organization has nothing to do except share the work of implementation. Bayley's model recognizes the importance of an effective crime-prevention component and technology that involves the community and the police.

There was the potential for a limited model of community policing in Seattle. Many citizens in low-income inner city neighborhoods lived in fear of guns, violence, and street crime. While the highest crime rates were within low-income communities and public housing dwellings, the potential for periodic unorganized and sporadic gunfire in downtown areas of large cities was ever-present.

A reformist model for community policing would require police officers and officials to get out of their cars and establish ongoing and meaningful relationships with the residents of their beats. This model for community policing, crime prevention, and crime control would require *equal* support from the mayor, the police chief, the city council, and community activists. This model would require that police live in the community they police and become more highly integrated into the community.

The rhetoric of community policing must be separated from the reality of community policing in practice. The wide gulf between the rhetoric and promises of community policing and what happens down on the streets and in central city neighborhoods has been documented. The optimal goal of the model would be that police would be required to live in the communities they police. They cannot be seen as an outside force that sweeps in only during times of conflict or increase of crime. They must be ever-present in the neighborhood and easily accessible to residents who are in need of assistance and service (Iadicola, 1988; Robinson et al., 1994).

Although the implications of this study are numerous, it best reflects the turbulent time period being researched (1985-1993). This period has been described by Michael Tonry (1995:209) as one of "malign neglect." Police and communities nationwide were called upon by political actors to do more with less about their crime problems. Most important, police executives and major political leaders called for the implementation of a policy to prevent civil disturbances and race and class conflicts. This policy was to be called "community policing." Community policing has come to mean different things to different people. This study explored one department's efforts to implement a version of this "new" policy.

Community policing has been highly political, as well as symbolic. In Seattle, community policing overemphasized rhetoric and fell short of the ideals visualized by experts. The politics of community policing were not the result of rational planning but the interaction between the community and neighborhood pressures and police department constraints. Although rarely discussed as departments implement their versions of this organizational philosophy, politics must be confronted when designing community policing in the future.

Appendix A

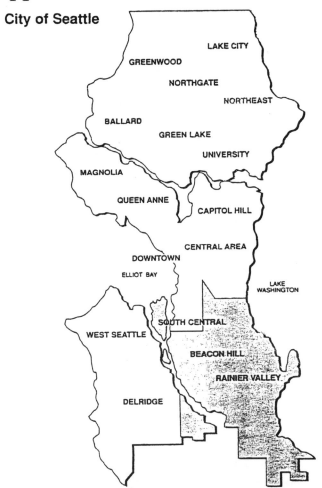

City of Seattle

**Figure A-1. Map of the City of Seattle, Washington. The SSCPC
target area is shown in gray.**

Adapted from National Institute of Justice Journal (August 1992) Community
Policing. Washington, D.C.: United States Department of Justice.

Appendix B

**SOUTH SEATTLE CRIME PREVENTION COUNCIL
(A.K.A. RAINIER CHAMBER OF COMMERCE) 15-POINT
PLAN FOR SOUTH SEATTLE (CENTRAL DISTRICT)**

1. The South Precinct Commander shall head the project. This person must be proactive and community oriented, a motivator, creative, and committed to community participation in the program. He/she must have total support from the Chief of Police, the Mayor, and the Community Advisory Committee to effectively implement the Program.

2. A Community Advisory Committee shall be established to work directly with the South Precinct to develop community support and monitor the program and establish guidelines. This Advisory Committee shall work closely with the Precinct Commander on all aspects relative to the reduction of crime in Southeast Seattle, understanding, of course, the confidential nature of police work. Members of the committee shall be selected from a cross section of Southeast residents and business people. The committee shall be representative of the socio-economic diversity of the area.

3. Three lieutenants (watch commanders) shall be assigned to the Project at the South Precinct. These lieutenants must have a working knowledge of the Program, must be able to work closely with the community, and must be committed to the basic concepts of the Program. Six patrol sergeants (three Robert and three Sam sector sergeants for three shifts) shall be

assigned. The sergeants should have the ability to motivate and aggressively lead officers in a pro-active effort.

4. These sectors shall be staffed with officers dedicated to the spirit of the Program.

5. Staffing: Eight patrol officers shall be reallocated from other police functions. This assignment is intended to increase the number of two-officer patrol units, directed accountable to the South Precinct Commander.

6. The staffing level of the anti-crime team shall be maintained. A clerk shall be assigned to the team.

7. The following staff shall be assigned to the South Precinct: Two detectives from the Narcotics Unit, one detective from the Commercial Unit, two juvenile detectives, two officers from the Special Patrol Unit (SPU), and an officer from the Crime Prevention Unit. All of these individuals shall be accountable to the Precinct Commander to be used as needed in this pilot project.

8. An incentive program shall be an option to be implemented at the South Precinct, at the discretion of the Captain.

9. Additional clerical assistance shall be provided from officers on limited duty, such as the CSO Unit, to free up, as possible, professional staff time from clerical duties.

10. Reasonable funds shall be committed for confidential informants and controlled narcotics buys.

11. The community will assist in recruiting "loaned" clerical workers, in purchasing equipment, and in locating space where the Police Department budget will not provide needed resources. This support activity will further include, but not be limited to, enlisting community support to work in and organize trouble areas as identified by police, secure office space if needed and be available, as needed, to coordinate with the Seattle Public Schools and local social services agencies.

12. Precinct personnel shall be trained to deal with selected problem areas in cooperation with the Community Advisory Committee to provide liaison between the community, the Committee, and the South Precinct.

13. A computer and software for tracking data from the two sectors, plus approximately $2,000 for miscellaneous equipment such as surveillance gear, shall be provided to the Program. If the Department has insufficient funds, the

community shall undertake a fund-raising campaign to pay for this equipment.

14. A total commitment to this Program from the Mayor and the Chief of Police is *CRITICAL* to the Program's success.

15. A total commitment from the Southeast community throughout the term of the Program is *also* essential to the Program's success.

While this project calls for deployment of resources from other units, they are services which are already utilized locally. However, they are currently neither easily accessible nor coordinated with the South Precinct. Localization of all personnel, appropriate services, and equipment is essential to streamline communications and produce results.

CONCLUSIONS

The Rainier Chamber of Commerce is committed to working with the City, local businesses and community groups to insure a significant reduction of crime in Southeast Seattle. Inherent in this Program is the assurance that the Southeast community *will* spend the time, locate the resources, and mobilize the community to implement this program.

Adapted from Fleissner, Dan, Fedan, Nicholas, Stotland, Ezra, and Klinger, David (1991) Community Policing in Seattle: A Descriptive Study of the South Seattle Crime Reduction Project. Seattle, WA: Seattle Police Department.

References

Albrecht, Stan, and Green, Miles. (1977) Attitudes toward the police and the larger attitude complex: Implications for police-community relationships. *Criminology,* 15(1): 67-86.

Alpert, Geoffrey P., and Dunham, Roger G. (1988) *Policing Urban America.* Prospect Heights, IL: Waveland Press, Inc.

Barnes, William R. (1990, June) Urban policies and urban impacts after Reagan. *Urban Affairs Quarterly 25, 4,* 562-573.

Bayley, David H. (1985) *Patterns of Policing.* Newark, NJ: Rutgers University Press.

Bayley, David H. (1988) Community policing: A report from the devil's advocate. In J.R. Greene and S.D. Mastrofski (Eds.), *Community Policing: Rhetoric or Reality* (pp. 225-237). New York: Praeger Publications.

Bayley, David H. (1994) *Police for the Future.* New York: Oxford University Press.

Beauregard, Robert A. (1993) *Voices of Decline: The Postwar Fate of U.S. Cities.* Cambridge, MA: Blackwell Publishers.

Bennett, W. Lance (1983) *News: The Politics of Illusion.* New York: Longman Inc. Bennis, Warren G., Benne, Kenneth D., and Chin, Robert (Eds.) (1969) *The Planning of Change* (2nd ed.). New York: Holt, Rinehart, and Winston.

Benveniste, Guy (1983) *Bureaucracy* (2nd ed.). San Francisco, CA: Boyd & Fraser Publishing Company.

Bereano, Philip L. (1993, Sept. 14) Headline appears to distort results of poll on police chief. *Seattle Times,* p. B1.

Birkland, Dave (1992, May 1) Youths rampage in downtown Seattle: Rice urges healing, not violence. *Seattle Times,* p. A1.

Birkland, Dave (1994, Feb. 13) Departing chief made a lasting impression. *Seattle Times*, p. B1.

Bouza, Anthony V. (1990) *The Police Mystique.* New York: Plenum Press.

Brogden, Michael (1982) *The Police: Autonomy and Consent.* New York: Academic Press.

Brogden, Michael, Jefferson, Tony, and Walklate, Sandra (1988) *Introducing Policework.* Boston: Unwin Hyman Ltd.

Brown, Lee P. (1985) Police-community power sharing. In W.A. Geller (Ed.), *Police Leadership in America: Crisis and Opportunity* (pp. 70-83). New York: American Bar Foundation.

Brown, Lee P. (1989, Aug.) Community policing: A practical guide for police officials. *Police Chief*, 72-82.

Brown, Lee P. (1993, Sept. 3) [Personal interview]. Unpublished raw data.

Brown, Lee P., and Wycoff, Mary Ann (1987) Policing Houston: Reducing fear and improving service. *Crime and Delinquency*, *33*(1), 71-89.

Brown, Michael K. (1981) *Working the Street: Police Discretion and the Dilemma of Reform.* New York: Russell Sage Foundation.

Brown, Robert (1992, Apr. 6) Weed and Seed problem is one of crime, not race [Letter to the editor]. *Seattle Times*, p. A11.

Brown, Damita, and Kratz, Amy (1992, Apr. 26) Weed and Seed grant money should be used to provide part-time jobs for youth [Letter to the editor]. *Seattle Times*, p. A19.

Cain, Maureen (1973) *Society and Policeman's Role.* Boston: Routledge & Kegan Paul.

Cain, Maureen, and Sadigh, Susan (1982, Summer) Racism, the police and community police: A comment on the Scarman report. *Journal of Law & Society*, *9*(1), 87-102.

Carter, David L., and Radelet, Louis A. (1994) *The Police and the Community* (5th ed.). New York: Macmillan College Publishing Company.

Carroll, Terrence (1993) Unpublished report.

Cashmore, Ellis (1991) Black cops inc. In E. Cashmore and E. McLaughlin (Eds.), *Out of Order: Policing Black People* (pp. 87-108) New York: Routledge, Chapman and Hall Inc.

Chambliss, William J. (1994, May) Policing the ghetto underclass: The politics of law and law enforcement. *Social Problems*, *41*(2), 177-194.

Couper, David C. and Lobitz, Sabine (1991, May) The customer is always right. *The Police Chief*, *58*(5), 16-21.

Criminal and Social Justice Associates (1994) The iron fist and the velvet glove. In Victor E. Kappeler (Ed.), The Police and Society. Prospect Heights, IL: Waveland Press, Inc.

Domhoff, G. William (1986, Spring) State autonomy and the privileged position of business: An empirical attack on a theoretical fantasy. *Journal of Political and Military Sociology*, 149-162.

Easton, David (1965) *The Political System*. New York: Knopf.

Eck, John E., and Rosenbaum, Dennis P. (1994) The new police order: Effectiveness, equity, and efficiency in community policing. In D.P. Rosenbaum (Ed.), *The Challenge of Community Policing: Testing the Promises*, (pp. 3-23). Thousand Oaks, CA: SAGE Publications, Inc.

Edelman, Murray (1977) *Political Language: Words that Succeed and Policies that Fail*. New York: Academic Press.

Elkin, Stephen L. (1987) *City and Regime in the American Republic*. Chicago, IL: University of Chicago Press.

Erie, Steven P. (1988) Big-city rainbow politics: Machines revividus? In S.P. Erie, *Rainbow's End: Irish-Americans and the Dilemmas of Urban Machine Politics, 1840-1985* (pp. 238-246). Berkeley, CA: University of California Press.

Evers-Aguilar, Chris (1992, Nov. 13) Weed and Seed plan won't solve all Central Area's problems, but it's worth a try [Letter to the editor]. *Seattle Times*, p. A9.

Fleissner, Dan, Fedan, Nicholas, Stotland, Ezra, and Klinger, David (1991) *Community Policing in Seattle: A Descriptive Study of the South Seattle Crime Reduction Project*. Seattle, WA: Seattle Police Department.

Fleissner, Dan, Fedan, Nicholas, Stotland, Ezra, and Klinger, David (1992, Aug.) Community policing in Seattle: A model partnership between citizens and police. *National Institute of Justice Journal*, 9-18.

Free, Marvin D., Jr. (1996) *African Americans and the Criminal Justice System*. New York: Garland Publishing, Inc.

George, Andrew James (1993) *The First Line Supervisor's Perspective of Community Policing: A Participant Observation Study*. Unpublished manuscript.

Gilroy, Paul (1982) Police and thieves. In Centre for Contemporary Cultural Studies (Ed.), *The Empire Strikes Back* (p.143-153). London: Hutchinson & Co.

Goldstein, Herman (1987, Jan.) Toward community-oriented policing: Potential, basic requirements, and threshold questions. *Crime and Delinquency*, *33*(1), 6-30.

Goldstein, Herman (1990) *Problem-Oriented Policing*. New York: McGraw-Hill.

Goldstein, Herman (1993, Aug. 24) *The New Policing: Confronting Complexity.* Paper presented at the Conference on Community Policing, National Institute of Justice, U.S. Department of Justice, Washington, D.C.

Gordon, Paul (1987) Community policing: Towards the local police state? In P. Scraton (Ed.), *Law, Order and the Authoritarian State: Reading in critical criminology.* Philadelphia: Open University Press.

Greene, Jack R., and Mastrofski, Stephen D. (1988) *Community Policing: Rhetoric or Reality.* New York: Praeger Publications.

Greenberg, David F. (1981) *Crime and Capitalism.* Palo Alto, CA: Mayfield Publications.

Gurr, Ted R. (1970) *Why Men Rebel.* Princeton, NJ: Princeton University Press.

Gusfield, Joseph R. (1963) *Symbolic Crusade: Status Politics and the American Temperance Movement.* Urbana, IL: University of Illinois Press.

Hall, Stuart, Critcher, Chas, Jefferson, Tony, Clarke, John, and Roberts, Brian. (1978) *Policing the Crisis: Mugging, the State, and Law and Order.* New York: Holmes & Meier Publishers.

Harrigan, John J. (1993) *Political Change in the Metropolis* (5th ed.). New York: Harper Collins College Publishers.

Harring, Sidney (1983) *Policing a Class Society.* Newark, NJ: Rutgers University Press.

Hartmann, Francis X., Brown, Lee P., and Stephen, Darrel (1988) *Community Policing: Would You Know it if You Saw it?* East Lansing, MI: National Neighborhood Foot Patrol Center, School of Criminal Justice, Michigan State University.

Iadicola, Peter (1988) *Neighborhood and Criminal Justice Strategies to Address Crime and Conflict: An Exploration of Areas of Intersection.* Unpublished manuscript.

Judd, Dennis R. (1988) *The Politics of American Cities: Private Power and Public Policy.* San Francisco, CA: Harper Collins Publishers.

Judd, Dennis, and Kantor, Paul (Eds.) (1992) *Enduring Tensions in Urban Politics.* New York: Macmillan Publishing Company.

Kappeler, Victor E. (Ed.) (1995) *The Police & Society.* Prospect Heights, IL: Waveland Press, Inc.

Kappeler, Victor E., and Kraska, Peter B. (1997) Policing modernity: Scientific and community based violence on symbolic playing fields. In Stuart Henry and Dragan Milovanovic (Eds.), *Constitutive Criminology at Work* (pp. 3-8). Albany, NY: SUNY Press.

Kappeler, Victor E., Sluder, Richard D., and Alpert, Geoffrey P. (1994) *Forces of Deviance: Understanding the Dark Side of Policing.* Prospect Heights, IL: Waveland Press, Inc.

Katznelson, Ira (1976) The crisis of the capitalist city: Urban politics and social control. In *Theoretical Perspectives on Urban Politics* (pp. 214-229). Englewood Cliffs, NJ: Prentice-Hall, Inc.

Katznelson, Ira (1981) *City Trenches*. New York: Pantheon Books.

Katznelson, Ira (1992) *Marxism and the City*. Oxford: Clarendon Press.

Kelling, George L. (1985) *Neighborhoods and Police*. Cambridge, MA: Harvard University Press.

Kelling, George L. (1987) *From Political to Reform to Community: The Evolving Strategy of Police*. Cambridge, MA: Harvard University.

Kelling, George L., and Bratton, William J. (1993, Jul.) Implementing community policing: The administrative problem. *Perspectives on Policing, 17*, 1-11. Washington, D.C.: National Institute of Justice.

Kennedy, David M. (1993) *Closing the Market: Controlling the Drug Trade in Tampa, Florida*. Washington, DC: National Institute of Justice.

Klockars, Carl B. (1985) *The Idea of the Police*. Beverly Hills, CA: SAGE Publications.

Klockars, Carl B. (1988) The rhetoric of community policing. In J.R. Greene and S.D. Mastrofski (Eds.), *Community Policing: Rhetoric or Reality* (pp. 239- 258). New York: Praeger Publications.

Klockars, Carl B. (1994) [Interview conducted by the New York City Police Police Executive Newsletter].

Lanier, Mark M. (1993) *An Examination of the Reliability and Validity of the Constructs Underlying Community Policing*. Unpublished manuscript.

Large, Jerry (1993, Mar. 20) Wanted: Officers who'll set roots where they serve. *Seattle Times*, p. B1.

Lehr, Kathi (1992, Apr. 6) Weed and Seed grant for Central Area is chance to support grass-roots efforts [Letter to the editor]. *Seattle Times*, p. A11.

Lilly, Dick (1992, Mar. 24) Attack crime or harass teens? Central District groups protest Weed and Seed grant. *Seattle Times*, p. B3.

Lilly, Dick (1992, Mar. 27) City urged to bury Weed and Seed plan—"They're gunning for Black youths," says teenager. *Seattle Times*, p. A1.

Lilly, Dick (1992, Apr. 6) Seattle wins grant for Weed and Seed program. *Seattle Times*, p. B1.

Lilly, Dick (1992, Apr. 7) Weed and Seed skeptics remain despite federal grant—Mayor still has to sell program to Central Area. *Seattle Times*, p. B1.

Lindblom, Charles A. (1977) *Politics and Markets: The World's Political Economic Systems*. New York: Basic Books.

Lipset, Seymour M. (1963) *Political Man*. New York: Doubleday.

Lipsky, Michael (1980) *Street-level Bureaucracy: Dilemmas of the Individual in Public Services.* New York: Russell Sage Foundation.

Lowi, Theodore (1969) *The End of Liberalism.* New York: W.W. Norton.

Manning, Peter K. (1977) *Police Work.* Boston: The Massachusetts Institute of Technology.

Manning, Peter K. (1984) Community policing. *American Journal of Police,* 3(2), 205-227.

Manning, Peter K. (1988) Community policing as a drama of control. In J.R. Greene and S.D. Mastrofski (Eds.), *Community Policing: Rhetoric or Reality* (pp. 27-45). New York: Praeger Publications.

Manning, Peter K. (1995) Economic rhetoric and policing reform. In V.E. Kappeler (Ed.), *The Police and Society* (pp. 375-391). Prospect Heights, IL: Waveland Press, Inc.

Mastrofski, Stephen D. (1988) Community policing as reform: A cautionary tale. In J.R. Greene and S.D. Mastrofski (Eds.), *Community Policing: Rhetoric or Reality* (pp. 47-67). New York: Praeger Publications.

Mastrofski, Stephen D. (1993) *The Impact of Community Policing at the Street Level: An Observational Study.* Unpublished manuscript.

McConville, Michael, and Shepherd, Dan (1992) *Watching Police, Watching Communities.* New York: Routledge.

McElroy, Jerome E., Cosgrove, Colleen A., and Sadd, Susan (1993) *Community Policing: The COP in New York.* Newbury Park, CA: SAGE Publications.

Michalowski, Raymond J. (1993) The contradictions of policing: An inquiry into nested dilemmas. In W.J. Chambliss and M.S. Zatz (Eds.), *Making Law: The State, the Law, and Structural Contradictions.* Bloomington, IN: Indiana University Press.

Miles, Jack (1992, Oct.) Blacks vs. Browns. *Atlantic Monthly,* 270(4), 41-68.

Moulakis, Athanasios (1985) *Legitimacy/Legitimate: Proceedings of the Conference held in Florence, June 3-4, 1982.* New York: Walter de Gauyter.

Nordlinger, Eric (1981) *On the Autonomy of the Democratic State.* Cambridge, MA: Harvard University Press.

Operation Weed & Seed Implementation Manual (1992) United States Department of Justice. Office of the Deputy Attorney General. Washington, D.C.

Peterson, Paul E. (1981) *City Limits.* Chicago, IL: University of Chicago.

Portland Police Bureau (1992) Community Policing Transition Information Packet. Portland, Oregon.

Portland Police Bureau (1994, March) Community Policing Strategic Plan. Portland, Oregon.

Radelet, Louis A. (1986) *The Police and the Community* (4th ed.). New York: Macmillan Publishing Company.

Ragin, Charles C., and Becker, Howard S. (1992) *What is a Case?* Cambridge, MA: Harvard University Press.

Reed, W. Edward (1995) *The Politics of Community Policing in Seattle, Washington (1985-1993)*. Unpublished doctoral dissertation, Northern Arizona University, Flagstaff.

Reiner, Robert (1985) *The Politics of the Police.* New York: St. Martin's Press, Inc.

Rice, Norm (1990, July 22) State of City speech.

Rice, Norm (1991, June 24) State of City speech.

Rice, Norm (1992, January 27) State of City speech.

Rice, Norm (1993, February 1) State of City speech.

Riechers, Lisa M., and Roberg, Roy R. (1990, June) Community policing: A critical review of underlying assumptions. *Journal of Police Science and Administration, 17*(2), 105-114.

Robinson, Cyril D., Scaglion, Richard, and Olivero, J. Michael (1994) *Police in Contradiction: The Evolution of the Police Function in Society.* Westport, CT: Greenwood Press.

Rodriguez, Matthew (1997, November) Community policing in Chicago. Paper presented at the Community Policing Strategies Conference, Dallas, TX.

Rosenbaum, Dennis P. (Ed.) (1994) *The Challenge of Community Policing: Testing the Promises.* Thousand Oaks, CA: SAGE Publications, Inc.

Saporito, Bill (1992, Nov. 2) The best cities for business. *Fortune,* 40-49.

Scheingold, Stuart A. (1990, Fall) University of Washington Political Science Publication.

Scheingold, Stuart A. (1991) *The Politics of Street Crime: Criminal Process and Cultural Obsession.* Philadelphia, PA: Temple University Press.

Scott, James (1990) *Community policing: A position paper.* Unpublished paper.

Scraton, Phil (1985) *The State of the Police.* London: Pluto Press.

Seattle District Attorney's Office Annual Report (1993) [unpublished report].

Seattle Police Department (1986) 1985 Annual Report. Seattle, WA: Academy Press.

Seattle Police Department (1987) 1986 Annual Report. Seattle, WA: Academy Press.

Seattle Police Department (1988) 1987 Annual Report. Seattle, WA: Academy Press.

Seattle Police Department (1989) 1988 Annual Report. Seattle, WA: Academy Press.

Seattle Police Department (1990) 1989 Annual Report. Seattle, WA: Academy Press.

Seattle Police Department (1991) 1990 Annual Report. Seattle, WA: Academy Press.

Seattle Police Department (1992) 1991 Annual Report. Seattle, WA: Academy Press.

Seattle Police Department (1992) 1991-1995 Long Range Plan: Partnership Policing in Seattle. Planning Section. Seattle, Washington.

Seattle Police Department (1993) 1992 Annual Report. Seattle, WA: Academy Press.

Seattle Police Department South Precinct. (1993, April 27). Unpublished internal memo.

Seattle Police Department (1994) 1993 Annual Report. Seattle, WA: Academy Press.

Seattle Police Department (1995) 1994 Annual Report. Seattle, WA: Academy Press.

Seattle Police Department (1996) 1995 Annual Report. Seattle, WA: Academy Press.

Seattle Times (1991, Aug. 9) p. A8.

Seattle Times (1992, Apr. 7) Weeding and Seeding: Local control key to success, support. p. A14.

Seattle Times (1992, May 1) p. A1.

Seattle Times (1994, Feb. 13) p. B1.

Selznick, Philip (1949) *TVA and the Grass Roots.* Los Angeles: University of California Press.

Sherman, Lawrence W., Milton, Catherine H., and Kelly, Thomas (1973) *Team Policing: Seven Case Studies.* Washington, D.C.: Police Foundation.

Skogan, Wesley G. (1990) *Disorder and Decline: Crime and the Spiral of Decay in American Neighborhoods.* New York: The Free Press.

Skolnick, Jerome H. (1971) *Politics of Protest.* New York: Ballantine Books.

Skolnick, Jerome H., and Bayley, David H. (1986) *The New Blue Line: Police Innovation in Six American Cities.* New York: The Free Press.

Sparrow, Malcolm K. (1988) Implementing community policing. *Perspectives on Policing.* Washington, D.C.: National Institute of Justice.

Sparrow, Malcolm K., Moore, Michael H., and Kennedy, David M. (1990) *Beyond 911: A New Era for Policing.* New York: Basic Books.

Stone, Clarence (1989) Urban Regimes: A Research Perspective. In C. Stone, *Regime Politics: Governing Atlanta* (pp. 3-12). Lawrence, KS: University of Kansas Press.

Strecher, Victor (1991) Revising the histories and futures of policing. *Police Forum*, *1*(1), 1-9.

Sykes, Gary (1986) Street justice: A moral defense of order maintenance. *Justice Quarterly*, *3*(4).

Taylor, Quintard (1994) *The Forging of a Black Community: Seattle's Central District from 1870 through the Civil Rights Era*. Seattle: University of Washington Press.

Thompson, E.P. (1975) *Whigs and Hunters*. Middlesex, England: Harmondsworth (Penguin Books).

Toch, Hans, and Grant, J. Douglas (1991) *Police as Problem Solvers*. New York: Plenum Press.

Toch, Hans, Grant, J. Douglas, and Galvin, Robert T. (1975) *Agents of Change: A Study in Police Reform*. New York: John Wiley & Sons.

Tonry, Michael (1995) *Malign Neglect—Race, Crime, and Punishment in America*. New York: Oxford University Press.

Trojanowicz, Robert C. (1989) *Preventing Civil Disturbances: A Community Policing Approach*. East Lansing, MI: National Center for Community Policing, School of Criminal Justice, Michigan State University.

Trojanowicz, Robert C. (1990, Oct.) Community policing is not police-community relations. *The FBI Law Enforcement Bulletin*, *59*(10), 6-11.

Trojanowicz, Robert C. (1991, Mar.) Community policing curbs police brutality. *Footprints: The Community Policing Newsletter*, 1-3.

Trojanowicz, Robert C. (1992, Winter/Spring) Preventing individual and systemic corruption. *Footprints*, *4*(1), 1-3.

Trojanowicz, Robert C. (1993, Apr. 16) [Personal interview]. Unpublished raw data.

Trojanowicz, Robert C., and Bucqueroux, Bonnie (1990) *Community Policing: A Contemporary Perspective*. Cincinnati, OH: Anderson Publishing Company.

Trojanowicz, Robert C., and Bucqueroux, Bonnie (1992) *Toward Development of Meaningful and Effective Performance Evaluations*. East Lansing, MI: National Center for Community Policing, School of Criminal Justice, Michigan State University.

Trojanowicz, Robert C., and Bucqueroux, Bonnie (1994) *Community Policing: How To Get Started*. Cincinnati, OH: Anderson Publishing Company.

Trojanowicz, Robert C., Pollard, Bonnie, Colgan, Francine, and Harden, Hazel. (1986) *Community Policing Programs: A Twenty-Year View*. East

Lansing, MI: National Neighborhood Foot Patrol Center, School of Criminal Justice, Michigan State University.

Walker, Samuel (1984) "Broken windows" and fractured history. *Justice Quarterly*, *1*, 57-90.

Walker, Samuel (1992) *The Police in America: An Introduction* (2nd ed.). New York: McGraw Hill.

Walker, Samuel, Spohn, Cassia, and DeLone, Miriam (1996) *The Color of Justice: Race, Ethnicity, and Crime in America.* New York: Wadsworth Publishing Company.

Walzer, Michael (1986) *Spheres of Justice: A Defense of Pluralism and Equality.* New York: Basic Books.

Wasserman, Robert, and Moore, Mark (1988) Values in policing. *Perspectives in Policing.* Washington, DC: National Institute of Justice.

Weatheritt, Mollie (1988) Community policing: Rhetoric or reality. In J.R. Greene and S.D. Mastrofski (Eds.), *Community Policing: Rhetoric or Reality* (pp. 153-175). New York: Praeger Publications.

Weber, Max (1947) *The Theory of Social and Economic Organizations.* New York: Free Press.

Websdale, Neil S. (1991) Disciplining the non-disciplinary spaces, the rise of policing as an aspect of governmentality in 19th century Eugene, Oregon. *Policing and Society*, *2*, 88-115.

Websdale, Neil S. (1994) Non-policing, policing and progressivism in Eugene, Oregon. *Policing and Society*, *4*, 131-173.

Williams, Frank P. III, and Wagoner, Carl P. (1995) "Making the police proactive: An impossible task for improbable reasons." In V.E. Kappeler (Ed.), *The Police and Society* (pp. 365-374). Prospect Heights, IL: Waveland Press, Inc.

Williams, Hubert, and Murphy, Patrick V. (1990, Jan.) The evolving strategy of police: A minority view. *Perspectives on Policing*, No. 13.

Williamson, Don (1992, Apr. 14) Weed and Seed: A problem or a solution? *Seattle Times*, p. A19.

Williamson, Don (1992, Apr. 19) Weed and Seed: Trusting others amid a rising tide of terror and death. *Seattle Times*, p. A19.

Wilson, Duff (1993, Jan. 17) State drug laws tilt against blacks. *Seattle Times*, p. B1.

Wilson, James Q. and Kelling, George L. (1982, Mar.) Broken windows. *The Atlantic Monthly*, *256*, pp. 29-38.

Wong, Stuart (1992, Apr. 6) *Seattle Times*, p. A11.

Wright, Eric Olin (1978) *Class, Crisis, and the State.* London: NLB.

Wycoff, Mary Ann (1988) The benefits of community policing: evidence and conjecture. In J.R. Greene and S.D. Mastrofski (Eds.), *Community Policing: Rhetoric or Reality* (pp. 103-120). New York: Praeger Publications.

Wysong, Earl, Aniskiewicz, Richard, and Wright, David (1994, Aug) Truth and DARE: Tracking drug education to graduation and as symbolic politics. *Social Problems, 41*(3), 448.

Yates, Donald L. (1993, Apr. 21-24) *Community Policing Problems.* Paper presented at the 35th Annual Conference of the Western Social Science Association, Corpus Christi, Texas.

Index

CURRENT ISSUES IN CRIMINAL JUSTICE

FRANK P. WILLIAMS III AND MARILYN D. MCSHANE
Series Editors